When Change is Set in Stone:

An Analysis of Seven Academic Libraries Designed by Perry Dean Rogers & Partners: Architects

Michael J. Crosbie
architectural critic

and

Damon D. Hickey
academic librarian

Association of College and Research Libraries
A Division of the American Library Association
Chicago, 2001

The paper used in this publication meets the minimum requirements of
American National Standard for Information Sciences–Permanence of
Paper for Printed Library Materials, ANSI Z39.48-1992. ♾

Library of Congress Cataloging-in-Publication Data
Crosbie, Michael J.
    When change is set in stone: an analysis of seven academic libraries designed by Perry Dean
    Rogers & Partners / Michael J. Crosbie and Damon D. Hickey.
        p. cm.
    ISBN 0-8389-8136-4 (alk. paper)
    1. Library architecture--United States. 2. Academic libraries--United States. 3. Perry
Dean Rogers & Partners. I. Hickey, Damon Douglas. II. Title.

Z679.2.U54 C76 2001
727'.827'0973--dc21

                                                                        2001016069

Printed on recycled paper.

Printed in the United States of America.

05 04 03 02 01   5 4 3 2 1

Table of Contents

Preface

This book is a unique opportunity to appraise carefully and to present seven college and university libraries designed by Perry Dean Rogers & Partners of Boston. The firm has been designing campus libraries for the past thirty years. These projects are the most recent in an oeuvre of some twenty-nine libraries designed and constructed for some twenty-seven colleges and universities around the country. The libraries in this book were designed and constructed over a twelve-month period (except Gault, which is the first of two libraries completed for the College of Wooster) for six different institutions. Thus, they represent some of the latest thinking about this complex building type, and demonstrate a wide variety of solutions. They include everything from brand new buildings, to renovations and additions to existing buildings, to projects in difficult urban locations. Within these seven libraries is nearly every type of design problem that architects and librarians are likely to encounter.

In years past, library programs were written prior to the engagement of an architect. In today's reality, however, conflicting institutional priorities and constraints of site and budget make the collaboration of both professions essential. To evaluate the success of the buildings presented in this book and to suggest trends for the future, the perspectives of both an academic librarian and an architectural critic are needed.

Michael J. Crosbie is an architectural critic who has written about the work of Perry Dean Rogers and Partners over the past fifteen years, including a number of the firm's libraries. Dr. Crosbie focuses on the architectural aspects of the projects, with particular attention to how the architects responded to the issues of context (both physical and institutional), and how the libraries reflect the unique aspects of the colleges and universities where they are located. He also relates an appreciation of themes evident in these libraries that one finds in other work by the architecture firm.

Damon D. Hickey, director of libraries at the College of Wooster in Wooster, Ohio, appraises each of the buildings in the context of how they function both as libraries and in other ways on their campuses. Dr. Hickey considers their symbolic significance, the ways in which they are shaped by new technologies, their functions as campus centers, factors unique to each institution, and how well they "work" as libraries. His comments are based upon site visits to each of the seven libraries, as well as discussions with staff, faculty, and administrators.

The authors wish to thank Perry Dean Rogers & Partners for making it possible to write about the firm's library work. Our special thanks go to Anne Johnson for overseeing the project. We would like also to thank the following individuals who gave their time generously: Halcyon Enssle, Cathy Tweedle, Fred Schmidt, and Camilla Alire at Colorado State University; Kristin Senecal, Sue Norman, and Julie Bockenstedt at Dickinson College; Diane Graves, Beth Harris, Elizabeth Dolittle, Margaret Airey, Michael Mansfield, and Tammy Baker at Hollins University; Jennifer Sias, Wendy Morehead, Arnold Miller, Allen Taylor, Monica Brooks, and Jan Fox at Marshall University; and Beverly Griesholder, Ann Sleeman, Peter Barslem, M. J. Tooey, and Frieda Wiese at the University of Maryland, Baltimore, and Alicia Kennedy for her editorial contributions. Finally, we wish to thank Hugh Thompson, director of publications at the Association of College and Research Libraries for his outstanding editorial work and his support for the book.

Introductions

Michael J. Crosbie, the architectural critic

In the beginning was the word. The word — whether in the form of ink smeared on sheets of wood pulp or ethereal bytes of electronic data casting shadows on a computer monitor — is the raison d'être of the university. By whatever means, the transfer of information and culture is the central task of the academy. If the word is hallowed, then the repository for it becomes, in a sense, the most sacred place on campus. Indeed, most great universities grew from a collection of books: Yale University, for example, was founded by a group of scholars and churchmen who gathered on a Connecticut village green to donate their books.

The word is central and its tabernacle, so often, is also central — physically, socially and culturally. The library has traditionally been the place where students and scholars come together, not only to exchange information, but also to socialize, to share the culture of the institution. Where better to place the library than at the very heart of the campus, in the most spatially prominent spot, from which the entire institution radiates? One has only to think of great college campuses such as the University of Virginia or Columbia University to see the college library at its most exalted. Even at small, modest institutions, the library is often on the highest knoll or at the termination of a long axis or housed in the largest, oldest, or most finely crafted building on campus.

As designers of academic libraries, Perry Dean Rogers & Partners realize the gravity of this building type. Because libraries are important buildings, designing them is usually rewarding. The library is often the university's signature building the one that may best reflect the institution and its aspirations, its face to the outside world. Special sites are reserved for the library, and the administration, faculty, staff, students, alumni, and trustees are all attentive to its design and creation. The library may set the tone and the architectural language for buildings that come after it, so that its design reverberates across campus. The library and its services often become important tools in the marketing of the university to prospective students and to future benefactors.

Timeless qualities aside, university libraries are in great flux. On any campus, the library is ground zero in the digital revolution, the place where we first glimpse the future of how information is stored and disseminated. Today the library is less of a place to stack the canon than a portal through which we can retrieve information from anywhere. The librarians' job becomes more complex. They need to be experts on the library's own collection as well as instructors about how to access information worldwide. They need to help students pan the Internet's gold from its dross. As teachers, the librarians' stature has increased tremendously.

The functions of the spaces within the library have also changed to certain degrees. The solitary scholar is disappearing and the study group has arrived. Libraries need to accommodate teams of students working closely with faculty on projects. Spaces that support this change comfortably, with links to the digital world and multimedia, can be seen clearly in the seven projects reviewed. Also new is the role of the library as a social space, with food and informal settings for discussion and socializing, complete (in some cases) with data ports. Because the computer has become indispensable in scholarship, many students go to the library to access one, and the library becomes a non-stop bustle of activity. Again, these services are important lures when competing with other universities for students. Balancing all these new uses and the library's traditional functions, makes their design more demanding today than ever before.

To bring the academic community into the design of its libraries, Perry Dean Rogers & Partners uses a technique called the "wall process" that it has refined over the past thirty years. Even before the design of the building begins to take form, the architects engage those who will work in these libraries in articulating what kind of a building they want. As the design develops, drawings and models are presented to those stakeholders for comment, and more adjustments are made. By the time the design is ready for construction, it is a reflection of what the architects have gained from the participation of those who would live with the consequences of form making.

What you will find in each of these seven libraries is an astute sensitivity to the numerous, often conflicting, needs they must satisfy. But beyond that, Perry Dean Rogers & Partners (whose work I have followed and written about for the past fifteen years) have not forgotten the library's central role. Responding to the history of the institutions and the importance of context, they create libraries that are worthy tabernacles for the word, no matter what its form.

Damon D. Hickey, the academic librarian

Librarianship may be the only profession that derives its name from a particular type of building, the library, which, in turn, derives its name from a particular physical object, the book. Quite literally, a librarian is one who takes care of books in a building designed to store them. Physicians and nurses are not hospitalians; attorneys are not courtians; and teachers are not schoolians. But librarians are, well, librarians.

Librarians will, of course, reply that our profession is changing and that we are perhaps more appropriately called information specialists these days. Information that is available electronically anywhere the user can "plug in" is indeed the great new fact of librarianship. Nevertheless, librarianship remains to a far greater degree than most others a building-related profession, and for this reason, librarians have a passionate interest in the buildings where they work. When the opportunity comes along to shape a new library building, this interest becomes particularly intense.

In August of 1999, I visited six college and university campuses, including my own, where new library buildings designed by Perry Dean Rogers & Partners of Boston had been completed within a twelve-month period. As a veteran of two such programs on my own campus (including a seventh library, the Flo K. Gault Library, completed in 1995), and having worked with these architects over an eight-year period, I was fascinated to see the unity-in-variety of these structures. I was struck that these buildings differed so greatly from one another, and that their differences were often the result of different visions of what a library built in the late 1990s should be. These different visions, in turn, sometimes had more to do with the priorities of the college or university administrations than with what the librarians/information specialists thought they should be.

Because the work of librarians is so closely connected with their buildings, they tend to forget that the construction of a new library is an important event in the larger life of a college or university, and that such an event may take on political and social significance far beyond traditional study, scholarship, and research. New academic library buildings are very expensive. Most college or university administrators will not raise the money for or oversee the construction of more than one in their careers. And whether the metaphor "heart of the college" is an accurate description of the library's role in the educational process, it remains powerful in the minds of faculty, students, trustees, and administrators alike. No matter how fascinating a laboratory, residence hall, student union, field house, classroom building, arts center, performance space, or office building may be, none can really lay claim to the "heart" metaphor in the way that a library can.

So the question becomes, what should this heart look like as academic institutions enter the third millennium? The answers to this question determine, literally, the shape of the building that gives the library profession its name.

The seven libraries I visited were:

1. Wyndham Robertson Library at Hollins University in Roanoke, Virginia, opened in the spring of 1999.

2. Health Sciences and Human Services Library at the University of Maryland, Baltimore, Maryland, opened in the spring of 1998.

3. Flo K. Gault Library for Independent Study at the College of Wooster in Wooster, Ohio (my own institution), opened in the Fall of 1995, and the renovation of the adjoining Andrews Library, completed the same year.

4. Waidner Library at Dickinson College in Carlisle, Pennsylvania, opened in the fall of 1998, and the renovation of the adjoining Spahr Library, completed the same year.

5. Morgan Library at Colorado State University in Fort Collins, Colorado, expanded and renovated and completed in January 1999.

6. Timken Science Library in Frick Hall, also at the College of Wooster in Wooster, Ohio (my own institution), opened in the Fall of 1998.

7. John Deaver Drinko Library at Marshall University in Huntington, West Virginia, opened in the fall of 1998.

Factors Affecting the Construction of new Academic Libraries

In reviewing these seven projects, I was able to isolate nine factors, each of which seemed to have shaped several projects:

1. The growing importance of electronics;
2. The shift from exclusively individual learning to individual-and-collaborative learning;
3. Community and institutional pride;
4. The emerging role of libraries as campus centers and information commons;
5. The need for less expensive ways to store print;
6. The importance of historical materials;
7. Differing concepts about staff-staff and staff-user relationships;
8. Uncertainty about the future; and
9. Site, budget, and design considerations.

Factors Affecting the Construction of New Academic Libraries

Damon D. Hickey, the academic librarian

1. The Growing Importance of Electronics

Electronic catalogs are ubiquitous in the academic library world, as are other electronic resources (such as indexes and abstracts, and increasingly, full-text), and are the starting point for almost any library search. It is not surprising, therefore, that all the libraries are wired for data, with computers instead of card catalogs. Several of the projects included computer classrooms and laboratories as well. Until wireless data transmission replaces wired transmission within buildings, new academic libraries are well-advised to wire everything in sight: carrels, lounge furniture, study tables, classrooms, and offices. But data wiring is not yet seen in the same way as electrical wiring when construction budgets are created. Like most architects in the 1980s and 90s, Perry Dean Rogers & Partners, for example, considered data wiring to be "technology"—part of the project cost but not of the construction cost. Not realizing this, some institutions assumed that data wiring, like electrical wiring, would be included in the construction budget and therefore failed to provide for it in the project budget.

The future of print storage of information is hotly-debated, but the majority of these projects suggest that academic institutions are already voting against it with their construction dollars. Four of the six institutions (Colorado State, Dickinson, Hollins, and Marshall) opened their new libraries with parts of their print collections in remote storage. The other two provided compact on-site storage for lesser-used materials. All recognize the necessity long-term to reduce the rate of physical growth of their collections through a combination of dense storage and electronic access. Hollins' and Marshall's libraries were conceived with the explicit expectation that electronic access would increasingly replace print storage.

Electronics are redefining the purposes of libraries. When library users can access library information electronically from any point on campus, and increasingly from anywhere in the world, why should they come to the library? One answer is to get help in finding the best information, or in finding good information quickly. Hence, the inclusion in several of these projects of data-wired classrooms and labs. But there are other answers as well: a social center (hence, the inclusion of coffee bars in three of the projects, plus porch rockers at Hollins), a collaborative-learning facility (hence, the inclusion of group study rooms in all the projects), a full-service computing facility where students can use library materials and also word-process their papers (hence, the inclusion at Marshall of an all-night computer lab with full word-processing and spreadsheet software available), a quiet study alternative to a noisy residence hall (hence, the inclusion at Wooster of Independent Study carrels for seniors, providing plenty of workspace, Internet connection, and comfort), a source of assistive technology for people with disabilities (hence, the inclusion of assistive technology labs at Marshall and UM-B), a campus showpiece (especially Marshall, UM-B, Hollins' "Hollins Authors Room," and

On-line public access on a stack floor at John Deaver Drinko Library, Marshall University.

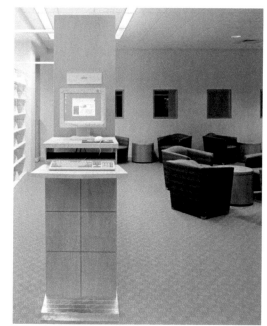

Wooster's Timken Science Library reading room), a technology center where all forms of information technology and staff are available (especially Marshall), a place to consult special collections and archives unique to each institution (most evident at Dickinson, UM-B, Hollins, and Wooster), or as a recruiting tool (for students, faculty, and staff).

Electronics have become a focus of interest for library users, donors, and prospective students, faculty, and staff. A high-tech library such as Marshall's is able to attract funds from donors and from the government. But even in less highly-technological libraries, computer laboratories provide "naming opportunities" for donors, and the presence of technology is often touted to prospective students, faculty, and staff as an indication that the institution is forward-looking.

In several of the libraries, especially Marshall's and UM-B's, electronics have shaped both the physical space and the administrative relationships among libraries, computing and other forms of information technology, and instructional media. Marshall's integration of these services is the most complete, while UM-B's is partial and in flux. In both, provision was made within the library buildings for technology offices and facilities. In other libraries, this provision was not made, meaning either that administrative merger will be less likely or that it will be more difficult, since it is more expensive to convert space designed for other purposes. At UM-B, last-minute decisions about what computing facilities to include led to an inconvenient arrangement of offices in spaces designed for other purposes.

The emphasis on electronics in teaching and learning had resulted in the transformation of print from the primary tool for teaching and learning to just one among many instructional technologies at some institutions. At Marshall, this transformation is particularly evident in a library that is only partially a print warehouse, and where distance-learning and large computer-presentation rooms are noticeable. At UM-B, the transformation is less obvious and less thorough. A distance-learning classroom, for example, has been equipped but is little-used.

2. The Shift from Exclusively Individual to Individual-and-Collaborative Learning

As ubiquitous as electronics in new libraries are group instruction rooms. All of these new libraries had them. UM-B, with a largely commuter student body engaged in the study of medicine, had the most (forty-two). Both UM-B's and Marshall's group studies are available in several levels of technological sophistication. All were data-wired, and some included televisions, VCRs, and computers as well. Clearly, the traditional image of the library as the hushed haven of the solitary scholar has changed.

A multi-media auditorium at the John Deaver Drinko Library, Marshall University.

Electronic classrooms and instructional labs were also nearly universal in these projects. The inclusion of these teaching and learning spaces is the result of two trends in higher education: (1) the trend toward collaborative learning and (2) digital technology's breakdown of barriers between print and electronics, between information ownership and information access, and between the library and the classroom/lab. In the past, new libraries sometimes included classrooms where teachers could bring their students for "bibliographic instruction." Now nearly every library is so technology-enhanced that it is only natural to include in new buildings the most up-to-date electronic teaching facilities. "Bibliographic instruction," which focused on the teaching of library research skills by librarians, has given way to "information literacy," which focuses on the integration of information-seeking and evaluation skills into classroom instruction by the faculty. From there it is only a short step to the library as a teaching center where faculty themselves receive instruction in how to enhance their teaching through the use of information technology. Of these projects, Marshall University's comes the closest to realizing this vision.

Distance learning is perhaps the ultimate form of collaborative learning, since it makes possible the real-time collaboration of teachers and learners separated physically from one another. Again, Marshall University's Drinko Library is the only one of these projects to have included a distance-learning classroom.

3. Community and Institutional Pride

Each of these projects attempts to make a bold but reassuring architectural statement. On every campus, the new libraries contain familiar elements of campus architecture: similar building materials, architectural ornamentation and decoration, fenestration, or scale. Colorado State, UM-B, and Marshall's libraries balance the familiar with the bold, especially in their use of strong color and their multi-story grand entrances. Wooster's Gault Library uses color, but in subtler ways; its bold stroke is its three-story glass façade and clock tower. Wooster's Timken Science Library transformed a dull back wall into a new façade with an entrance that simultaneously echoed the west façade of Andrews Library. Its grand reading room is a restoration of a nineteenth-century space, bringing back the intense colors that had been dulled-down by the twentieth century. At Dickinson, the use of color is more subdued and the library entrance is not as imposing from the outside as in the other projects, but the multi-story lobby with its clock wall makes a grand statement to anyone who enters. Reassurance is present in the myriad of nooks and crannies that are found in most of these buildings: spaces that have a very private feeling but that also at times startle and delight with unexpected vistas and colors.

Two of these libraries function in different ways as anchors for community development. The University of Maryland-Baltimore's project has helped to anchor Baltimore's West Side empowerment zone, reaching out to residents of the community in a variety of ways. Marshall University's library, likewise, plans to "extend its capabilities and outreach…to public schools, businesses, hospitals, other libraries, alumni, and area residents," primarily through the use of instructional technology and distance education.

It should not surprise librarians—but often does—that college and university administrators expect new libraries to be showpieces that make a statement to the community about the significance of the institution. One librarian commented to me that she was glad that her president had left because that meant that he would not be having receptions in the lobby anymore. Another librarian commented on how frustrating it was that the administration seemed unconcerned about the impact of "special events" held in the building on people who were studying there. Most librarians would probably want the library to be seen as important, but they usually mean that they want its educational and bibliographic functions to be paramount. Stunning architecture, dramatic spaces, and high tech are not what they usually mean, but they are what administrators use to impress outsiders. Why do libraries need sculpture inside the building (Colorado State), dramatic entrances (all), sweeping staircases (especially UM-B), intense colors on serpentine walls (UM-B, Colorado State, and Marshall), multi-story glass walls (Gault at Wooster), clock towers or clock walls (Gault at Wooster, Dickinson), coffee shops (UM-B, Marshall, Hollins), board rooms (UM-B), dramatic classical reading rooms (Timken at Wooster), or wireless hand-held computers (Marshall)? They don't, but these enhancements make the statements about institutional significance that every administrator longs for.

Parallel to the library's function of reassuring while challenging through bold innovation, several of these libraries' architecture integrate past and future. That is not surprising, since most libraries comprise a pre-fifteenth-century information technology (handwritten manuscripts), a fifteenth-century technology (printing), and twentieth-century technologies (film, video, and digital media). Wooster's Timken Science Library is the most notable example, combining a late-nineteenth-century building that was itself an architectural homage to the history of western culture with the dramatically-different technologies of the late twentieth century. Likewise, Hollins' new library resembles its early-nineteenth-century buildings and celebrates the university's literary heritage, while simultaneously trying to be as up-to-date as possible. At both Dickinson and Wooster, a new library building was added to an old one, transforming both into something both familiar and new. Colorado State literally wrapped a new library building around an old one.

Circulation desk lounge as seen from reading balcony at Waidner Library, Dickinson College.

One library staff member joked that whenever the college administration referred to something as an "admission tool," it was almost certainly a bad idea. But new libraries are, deliberately or not, tools for recruiting faculty, staff, students, and money. Marshall's new building attracted a great deal of money, from both private and public sources. UM-B personnel candidly admitted that they were able to get better staff without raising salaries because of their new building. Wooster's science faculty saw their new science library as a drawing card for prospective faculty and students. Wooster's Gault Library was built in part to attract students by giving Independent Study a physical expression.

4. The Emerging Role of Libraries as Campus Centers and Information Commons

As noted previously, the advent of electronics has served to highlight and even to enhance the non-library-research uses of libraries. All of the buildings studied provide comfortable and varied spaces for users in cheerful, bright, and often colorful settings. Wooster's Gault Library, for example, provides study carrels that are tucked away, study carrels in a loft setting, study carrels by windows, study carrels in high-traffic areas, lounge seating, and study tables. Dickinson's new library provides dramatic vistas of the campus from carrels, tables, easy chairs, and window seats. Both Hollins and Colorado State feature picture-window reading rooms

that look out upon mountains (the Blue Ridge and the Rockies, respectively), but provide as well solitary nest-like loft seating along with the full range of other types of study areas. The aim is to accommodate nearly every taste and preference, so that every library user can have his or her own favorite place to read, study, and even nap.

Hollins, Marshall, and UM-B, taking a page from the large bookstore chains, provide cafés and lounges, where students may find refreshment without having to leave the building, while simultaneously banning food and drink from the library proper.

The main reading room at Timken Science Library, College of Wooster. One of the new mezzanines is seen on the right.

12

Timken Science Library,
The College of Wooster.

To a greater or lesser extent, all of these libraries, especially Marshall, provide public computing facilities, some with extended hours. In Marshall's case, some public computing was actually shifted from elsewhere on campus to the new library.

All of the new libraries have become places where public events—receptions, board meetings, lectures, exhibits—take place. Hollins' Hollins Authors Room was designed for just this sort of event, and is scheduled by an office outside the library. The Board Room at UM-B is where the university's trustees meet. The main reading room in Wooster's Timken Science Library has been the venue for a variety of campus receptions, as have the lobbies and reading rooms of several other libraries. Special Collections spaces are often used to show off treasures of these libraries, as are special exhibit areas, such as that just inside the entrance to Colorado State's library. Colorado State also provides space for large, dramatic works of sculpture.

At Marshall and to a lesser extent at UM-B, offices, equipment, and staff for information technology are incorporated into the design of the libraries, thereby creating a sort of "information commons" for the campuses.

5. The Need for Less Expensive Ways to Store Print

Libraries were once built to house all the books and periodicals a college or university would ever expect to acquire. The College of Wooster's first library building (now its science library) was expected to have this sort of useful life. In fact, it served the institution's needs for sixty years. Its successor library was good for only thirty. The complex of three libraries at Wooster as

of the year 2000, including both of the older buildings, was designed to provide only fifteen years of growth. In other words, each new building has extended the useful life of its predecessors by only half of their original lifespan. All of these libraries reflect that trend, with growth space for print ranging from ten to twenty years. In several cases, the projected useful life of the building assumes that some materials will remain permanently housed off-site.

All of these library collections are divided into materials that are used more often and are therefore kept more readily available and those that are expected to have lower use and are therefore less accessible. At

Third floor reading area at Wyndham
Robertson Library, Hollins University.

UM-B and Wooster, this division is represented simply by the use of mobile compact shelving for some materials, whereas in others the lesser-used materials are stored somewhere other than the new library, with as much as a day needed for them to be retrieved. (At Marshall the original intent was to close the stacks of the old library and make materials stored there available after one day's wait, but more recently the administration has decided to continue to make these materials available directly to users by staffing and renovating the old library building.) UM-B has yet to use its compact shelving, which is available once the regular stacks fill up. Several other libraries built floors capable of holding the weight of compact shelving if needed in the future.

This division of library collections assumes in general that newer is better, since it is usually the newer books or periodicals that are in the new libraries, while the older ones are in storage or compact shelving. There is, therefore, an implicit hierarchy of information: electronically-stored information, which is generally the most recent, is the most available. Recently-published print material is the next-most-recent and is, therefore, available on open shelves. Older materials that are needed frequently are often maintained in microform, which is harder to use than either digitally-stored materials or print. And still older materials that are needed the least find their way into compact shelving (which is on-site, but is more difficult to use than conventional open shelving) or into a remote storage facility, to be retrieved upon demand. Since ease of accessibility usually correlates with frequency of use, the consignment of lesser-used materials to less-accessible locations means that these materials will be used even less than they would have been on open shelves or in digital form. The bias toward material that is more current and therefore easier to retrieve is therefore reinforced by this division of library collections—a fact that will surely have an impact on education and research in the future.

The Special Collections Reading Room at Health Sciences and Human Services Library, University of Maryland-Baltimore.

6. The Importance of Historical Materials

Running counter to the trend toward making older library materials less available is the trend, visible in several of these new libraries, toward special care and visibility for materials that are very old, very rare, or very important to the history of the college or university. New or expanded, climate-controlled spaces, with associated areas for exhibit and rooms in which readers and researchers can use these materials under the watchful eye of staff are found in several of these projects. Wooster's renovation of space in Andrews Library and Marshall's renovation of space in its old library for special collections, Hollins' special collections and its Hollins Authors Room, Dickinson's dramatic special collections room and its exhibits of

artifacts associated with its Priestly Collection, and UM-B's special collections all underscore the growing importance of these special and archival collections to their institutions, emphasizing as they do the unique character, history, and importance of each institution. Futurist John Naisbitt has written about the ways in which new trends evoke their opposites. Perhaps this passion for preserving the early records of institutions and cultures is an example of Naisbitt's thesis, an evocation of the hand-written and print record of the past occasioned by the ubiquity of "virtual" information.

New stairs to reading mezzanines as seen from the reference collection at Timken Science Library, The College of Wooster.

7. Differing Concepts about Staff-Staff and Staff-User Relationships

The directions in which library design has moved as a result of the foregoing trends has been much the same from library to library, with the primary difference being the speed of movement. But there is no clear single trend directing how staff are to be related to other library staff or to their users. One might assume that, given the trend toward collaborative learning, something similar might be at work here as well. But these building projects reflect not a single trend, but a continuation of existing practices and patterns. At Dickinson, librarians wanted to be readily accessible to both users and other members of the library staff, and were willing to give up exterior windows in order to be available to both. At Wooster, librarians wanted to be more remote from library service points so that they could have more privacy when not on "public duty." At UM-B, concerns similar to those at Wooster plus security concerns in an urban environment meant that staff who were not on duty in public service areas were literally locked away from the public. Even stranger, rather than taking all or part of a floor for staff, where individuals and departments could be kept together and close to others with whom they needed to interact frequently, UM-B put all staff offices along one long wall of the building on each floor—an arrangement that divided departments and divisions and made communication difficult. Even at Marshall, where various instructional technology and library departments are being integrated, the old divisions are enshrined in concrete, with different kinds of staff on different floors. If there is a trend here, it seems to be that, with the possible exception of Dickinson, staff who have been crowded together in old buildings for a long time, in non-functional ways, want their own spaces, their own windows, and greater privacy, even if that means that their new relationships are not much more functional (sometimes less so) than they were before. The most common complaint I heard from staff in these new libraries was, "I never see anyone anymore. Before, it seemed as though it was easy to see everybody. Now I have to make a conscious effort to go around and visit if I don't want to be isolated." Perhaps this is an example of being careful what one wishes for, because one might get it.

There seems also to be no clear pattern about optimal physical relationships between library staff and other, especially computing and instructional media. In none of these libraries were they fully integrated. At Marshall and UM-B they were physically proximate. Elsewhere they were almost totally separated. At Wooster, Computing runs the computer lab even though it is headquartered elsewhere, while at Dickinson there is someone from Computing on the library staff. The lack of uniformity and integration suggests that these relationships are still in flux, and that it will be some time before patterns develop.

Readers in Special Collections can be seen from a principal corridor at the Health Sciences and Human Services Library, University of Maryland-Baltimore.

A bridge above the double-height lobby at the Health Sciences and Human Services Library, University of Maryland-Baltimore.

8. Uncertainty about the Future

As noted above, uncertainty about the direction of administrative relationships can play havoc with library design. At UM-B in particular, one model of the relationship between library staff and computing staff was in operation when the library was designed, but was replaced by another too late to make appropriate design changes. As a result there is one office in the building that could just as well be somewhere else. Another set of offices is in spaces not well-suited to needs and is split up into different parts of the building. And the administrative suite has fewer occupants than it was originally designed to hold.

No one knows how fast digital media will replace print, which forms of print will be replaced and which will remain. Electronic periodicals may replace paper periodicals, but will e-books replace paper books? If they do, which titles will need to be acquired in paper form? Will libraries even be places in the future, or will most information be available online, with information literacy integrated into course instruction (digitally mediated?), and with all print materials stored in a central warehouse, with minimal duplication of titles, for pickup and delivery to library users wherever they reside? Institutions can plan only as far as they can see ahead. All that seems certain is that change will rule, and that it will move faster than expected and in unexpected directions. How long these seven libraries will be adequate to serve their institutions, therefore, is anyone's guess.

Similarly, no one knows whether or how much computers will reduce space needs. Should new libraries plan lots of rooms of different sizes for instruction and consultation, using a variety of instructional technologies? Should they data-wire everything that does not move, or should they plan to go wireless? Should they provide lots of public computers, or assume that everyone will have his or her own laptop? Wooster's Gault Library includes 285 senior carrels, each data-wired, based upon the assumption that students will opt increasingly for portable computers. Marshall, on the other hand, is checking out small, wireless computers that can go anywhere in the building and do anything that most desktop units can do.

What will future staffing patterns look like? No one seems to know. There seems to be a trend in higher education toward appointing chief information officers to oversee libraries and instructional technology, but the degree of integration of the services varies widely among institutions with a CIO. Librarians and other staff at Marshall, Hollins, UM-B, and Dickinson expressed similar uncertainty about these future staffing patterns, and some anxiety about how they would affect the library and its services. Needless to say, any major change in staffing patterns would have unforeseen implications for the use of space in the libraries.

9. Site, Budget, and Design Considerations

Most libraries, whether new buildings, renovations, or additions are constrained by their sites, including any existing building or buildings on those sites. Thus, Gault Library at Wooster could not go any farther north than the main classroom building next door, nor any higher or wider than Andrews Library, to which it was attached. Drinko Library at Marshall could not be attached to the existing buildings, all of which opened onto a plaza. Robertson Library at Hollins was nestled into the side of a hill. UM-B had an entire block in one dimension, but not in the other, forcing it into a rectangle rather than a square. Morgan Library at Colorado State was an existing L-shaped building, which the architects tried to make more functional as they added to it. Timken Science Library at Wooster was constrained by an existing library building to which nothing was added save a new entrance, although the stack wing was gutted and completely rebuilt.

Budget is undoubtedly the largest constraint faced by both building planners and architects. Rarely is enough money available to do everything that everyone would like to do, even given the ideal site. It played a major role in all of these projects. As a result of budget constraints, for example, the libraries at Hollins, Dickinson, Colorado State, and Marshall included many amenities and innovations, but not enough space to house their existing book collections plus growth space for the future. Indeed, only UM-B's library was designed with sufficient room for more than fifteen years of collection growth at existing rates of growth. At Wooster, budget constraints meant that the existing Andrews Library was renovated only minimally: a computer lab, a handicap entrance ramp, and improvements to the lower basement were among the items "value engineered" (construction-speak for "cut") out of the building program.

The section on "Community and Institutional Pride" detailed some of the design factors that shape libraries. Design considerations range from wanting the library to fit in with existing campus architecture to wanting the library to stand out from other buildings. But not all design considerations are of this sort. Few architects—and indeed, few colleges and universities—want to design and build libraries that are nothing more than warehouses for books. So they may create open stairways that give a feeling of space and movement, but may also transmit sound (as at Hollins). They may include atriums or courtyards, which may provide openness and light, but which eat up floor space, may create heating and cooling problems, and introduce sunlight that may contribute to the deterioration of paper.

Staircase at the Wyndham Robertson Library, Hollins University.

Questions and Tips for the Planner

the academic librarian

As someone who has been through the design and building process for two libraries at my present institution and for one at another institution, and who has had the opportunity through these visits to look at five other recently-built libraries, I want to give you, the reader, some questions to ask yourself, and some advice. Libraries that are built after this book is published will look in many respects very different from those described here. If I am correct in my identification of trends, newer buildings will reflect their influence even more than these projects did.

Expect electronics to be very important in the future in every way, and anticipate that your institution's administrators may not see that future in the same way as you or the teaching faculty do. Unfortunately, neither librarians nor teaching faculty have much clout when it comes to fundraising, and so it may be the administration's, and to some extent the trustees', vision that will shape your building. Does your institution have a chief information officer? Is it planning to get one? What is the relationship between the library, media services, and computing? What would you like it to be? How can you use the building program either to promote change or to slow it? Also, be certain that your project budget includes all the costs of electronics: hardware, wiring, routers, switches, and the like. If you plan to have electronic classrooms, be certain that you have all the equipment you need in the budget, with some provision for regular upgrades and replacements on some realistic cycle (three-to-five years).

What kinds of group study spaces will you need, and how many? Do you need several data-wired classrooms for library instruction, or do you expect the instruction to move into the classroom? What kind of program of information literacy do you have, and how will that impact the spaces you will need? What kinds of electronic and audiovisual equipment, if any, do you plan to put into group study rooms? Will you put the same thing in all rooms, or just in some? Will all or some or none of these rooms be available only by advance reservation?

What kinds of concessions are you willing to make to community and institutional pride? Are you willing to give up some space for public functions, art galleries, writing centers, lecture rooms, exhibit halls, or other spaces in order to get more of what you want in the library? And what is the trade-off? How much can be spent for these non-library matters without seriously eroding the funds available for library matters? Or will their inclusion enhance overall fundraising potential? How much disruption are you willing to live with in order to keep your administration's sense of "ownership" in the building after it opens? How bold and imaginative are you and your administration willing to be when it comes to design? How conservative? Are you going to have to add on to an existing building? If so, what opportunities and problems does that present?

Are you wedded to the idea of libraries for library research only, or are you willing to tolerate—even encourage—the use of the library for general study, as a social center, for general computer use, or for all-night study or computer use? Does the thought of a coffee bar in the building attract or repel you? What do your students say they want to see in the building? Is there a faculty lounge on campus? Would the new library be an appropriate place for one?

If you are interested only in getting a building big enough to hold all the print you hope to acquire in the next twenty-five years, at existing rates of growth, you are probably being unrealistic. On the other hand, if you fail to provide as much space for print volumes as possible in the building, you may never get another chance. If you can persuade your administration to install compact shelving on any floor that can bear the load, do it now, before you have filled the space with conventional shelving loaded with books that will have to be removed in order to install compact shelving later. In any event, you should be thinking about how you can use electronics to slow the growth of print, and about where you might store lesser-used materials (either compact shelving on-site or other spaces off-site) if that becomes necessary, and asking your administration for the necessary funds. If you are convinced that conventional open stacks are the only way for a library of the future to go, be prepared for an uphill battle.

What kinds of facilities for archives and special collections do you have now, and what do you and the administration want? Can you justify a very nice space for them based upon the ways in which they could be used in teaching? Can you sell to your administration the idea of preserving the institution's memory through an archives program? Do you have a collection development policy for special collections that will protect you from unforeseen large donations of materials for which you will have neither staff nor space? How much staff will you have, and how will they be able to serve the public? Will special collections have regular hours, or hours by appointment only? Are you prepared to take this on as a new cost center if it is not one already? Are there donors who might be attracted to underwriting such a project? What kinds of environmental controls do you need? What kind of public space do you need for users? For exhibits? For lectures and special events? What kind of storage space, processing space, and staff space do you need?

Based upon your library program, your workflow, your staff's interactions with your library users, and your relationships (present or hoped-for) with instructional technology staff, how should your staff be configured physically? And if some or all of that changes, will you have the flexibility to move people to where they need to be? Of course, everyone will want a window. Some individuals will want privacy, while others will want to be in a big room where they can see everyone else. But do you really want these sorts of considerations to determine your staff configurations? Ask your staff whether it is more important to give everyone a window, or to keep departments together. Use the opportunity of a new building to raise the issue of whether library and computing staff people should be closer to one another in order to facilitate cooperation. Try to plan staff locations in such a way that staff will meet and interact with one another naturally, in the course of their everyday activities, rather than have to go out of their way to see one another.

- How flexible can you make your building?
- Involve yourself and your staff as much as possible in the planning process, beginning with the selection of an architect. Find out how prospective architects will involve your staff in their planning. It they cannot describe a process that is truly inclusive, look for another architect. Plan to stay involved throughout the process. If you are not willing or able to keep track of the myriad details involved in design and construction, find someone on your staff who can and will, and make certain that that person keeps you apprised.
- Decide which battles you must win, and which you are willing to negotiate—or even concede. Which issues are library issues as opposed to aesthetic issues? If the only way you can get a new library is to let your institution build space in it for the Registrar's Office, or an art gallery, or instructional computing, can you accept that with good grace? In other words, where will you draw the line?
- If you are a new library administrator, coming into the middle of a building program, find out as much as you can from the architect and anyone else who has been involved as to what the planning assumptions are. For example, was the library planned to hold all your existing materials with no growth room, based upon the assumption that your collection would be steady-state in size, and are you willing to make that assumption? Or will you need to plan some off-site storage for lesser-used materials in order to have room for the collection to grow?
- Make certain that all elements of the project, including data wiring and any equipment and furniture that you will need, are included in the project budget.

If you are about to undertake this voyage, I wish you bon voyage and much joy. Building a new library may be one of the most exciting experiences of your career. May it also be one of the most satisfying!

Wyndham Robertson Library
Hollins University

the architectural critic

The new Wyndham Robertson Library at Hollins University in Roanoke, Virginia, is a place for the reverence of books, and those who write them. Hollins, which is the oldest women's educational institution in the state, is the alma mater of several noted writers, among them Mary Wells Ashworth and Annie Dillard. The school also claims Margaret Wise Brown, whose *Goodnight Moon* is a children's classic, and the school's graduate program in children's literature honors that tradition. Thus, at Hollins, the library is a setting for the launching of authors, as much as it is a facility with state-of-the-art technology for the pursuit of scholarship.

The mantel of tradition rests just as heavily on the campus and its architecture as it does on the written word. Hollins was founded in 1842, nestled in the foothills of the Blue Ridge Mountains. The oldest portion of the campus, listed on the National Register of Historic Places and known as the "Front Quad," is occupied by three-story, rectangular buildings clad in warm red brick; white-painted wood columns, porches, and trim; and low-sloped gable roofs. The size and proportion of the buildings' fenestration is classical and elegant.

Hollins' refined Georgian buildings serve as the progenitors of the new library, which is sited not far from the Front Quad, to the northeast, to form the east side of a new quadrangle. The building stretches north-south, opening its west side to views of the new quad and the older buildings beyond, while its east elevation frames views of the mountains.

Entrance façade.

The west elevation bears the strongest resemblance to the campus'; architectural pedigree. As are the university's most venerable buildings, the new library is three stories and rectangular, with an exterior of warm brick, white trim, an entrance portico in the spirit of Hollins' West Building of 1820. The windows have the same shape and portion of the older buildings, and in fact replicate the diamond-patterned glass on the old Cocke building—the campus' original library. Providing a strong visual base, a loggia of Tuscan columns stretches across the lower part of the facade. The ensemble of elements old and new results in a building that is faithful to the university's architectural tradition, and allows the new library to fit seamlessly into the campus.

The library's basement level contains storage spaces, stacks, multimedia rooms, a small auditorium, and study carrels. The second and third levels are devoted stacks, meeting spaces, administrative offices, single study carrels along the west walls, and a wealth of spaces for group study.

Third floor reading area with views to countryside beyond.

View to main stair from second floor.

First Floor Level

1. Reference Desk
2. 24 hour Commons
3. Circulation Desk
4. Reading Room
5. Book Stacks
6. Study Rooms
7. Reading Carrels

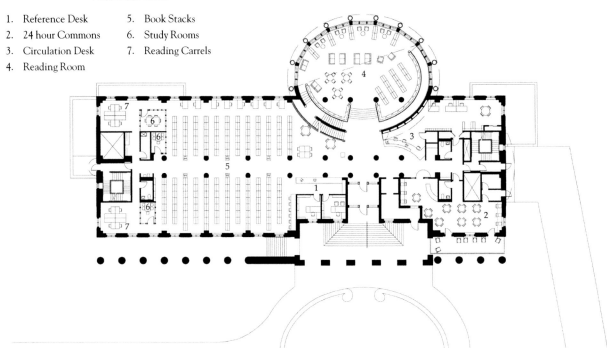

Periodicals reading room.

It is the first level, however, where the new library sings. One penetrates this bibliophile's jewel box on the west facade, up a grand set of stairs. Through the entry, one arrives at the heart of the library with its circulation desk and grand entrance to the oval reading room, with its view of the mountains. This space, wrapped in a curved wall of windows, is the library's gem, set as it is in the rectangular armature of the building. Circulation throughout the library wraps the western edge of the oval reading room in a gracious staircase that suggests the front hall of a Southern mansion. To the north are stack spaces and study rooms; to the south are administration spaces and a comfortable lounge outfitted with computer access. Throughout the building are display areas for art and the literary works of Hollins graduates.

The effect of this library has been positive on those students, faculty, and staff who use it. They comment most positively and frequently on its wealth of light and use of color, which make this environment "energizing, while maintaining its elegance," according to library director Diane Graves. It is an open, welcoming place, where students and faculty come not only to study and research, but also to browse and read, enjoy a cup of coffee, or play a game of chess.

While criticisms have focused on the noise level in this building of hard surfaces, and light fixtures difficult for relamping, it has received high praise. The library's most progressive elements, Graves notes, are its public spaces, such as the coffee commons, media commons, and art display areas. These features balance against the contextual spirit of its exterior, resulting in a building that "sends a high-tech message to those who seek state-of-the-art," while at the same time reassuring those who believe that the book is still central to the library. It demonstrates, notes Graves, that a building can be useful and beautiful, honoring tradition while accommodating change.

Double-height periodicals reading room with reading balcony above.

the academic librarian

Having experienced a disastrous flood that inundated its library, Hollins University (formerly Hollins College) had as its first requirement for a new library that it not be built in a flood plain. Its second requirement was that it be compatible with the architecture of the older campus buildings. These two requirements express nicely the library-functional side of library design and the non-library institutional side, respectively.

The new library is indeed above the flood plain, located on a rise just above and to the side of the chapel. The building also has emergency flood protection pumping systems. Hollins is nestled in the Blue Ridge Mountains, and its motto, Levavi Oculos ("Lift thine eyes"), are the opening words of Psalm 121, "I will lift up mine eyes unto the

View from Campus Ring Road.

hills." Whereas Hollins women and men at worship in the chapel could formerly lift their eyes to the Blue Ridge Mountains, now they "levavi their oculos" to the library! Stylistically, the library closely resembles the older buildings on the main quadrangle: red brick, white columns, Chinese-Chippendale-inspired railings, and even a porch with dark green rocking chairs.

The objective for the building's interior was to return student-centered study space to the library. In the old building, people got what they needed and left. Hollins wanted a library in which they would stay. During the summer session of 1999, half of the study space in the building was in use, indicating that the school's objective had been achieved. Hollins is primarily a women's institution, and so seating that has visual access to other areas provides a sense of security to female students. The building is well-lit, in contrast to the old building. Color, a characteristic of most Perry Dean Rogers & Partners buildings, helps to enliven this building. Each end room, for example, is a different color from those on other floors. These rooms are visible at night from the exterior, providing a rainbow effect.

A special feature of the new building is the Hollins Authors Room. Hollins has a distinguished history as a producer of authors, a history that earned the new library designation as a National Literary Landmark by the American Library Association. The Hollins Authors Room preserves the works of these outstanding alumnae, while functioning also as a space for general study, as well as university receptions and poetry readings. Outside the Hollins Authors Room is the Friendship Colonnade, a tribute to the lifelong friendships formed among Hollins women during their student days. Above it is a cozy Reading Loft accessible only by a spiral staircase.

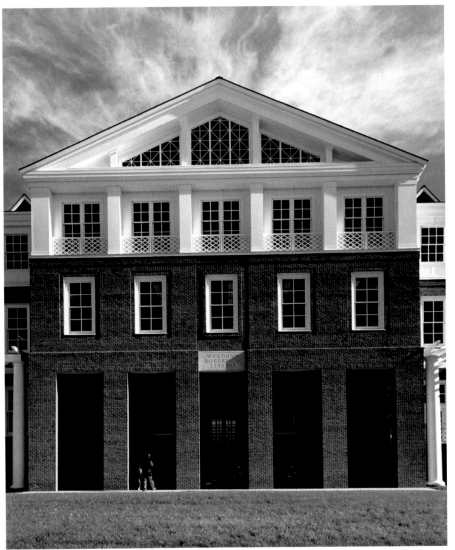

Entrance portico.

View from existing main quadrangle with chapel in foreground.

North façade.

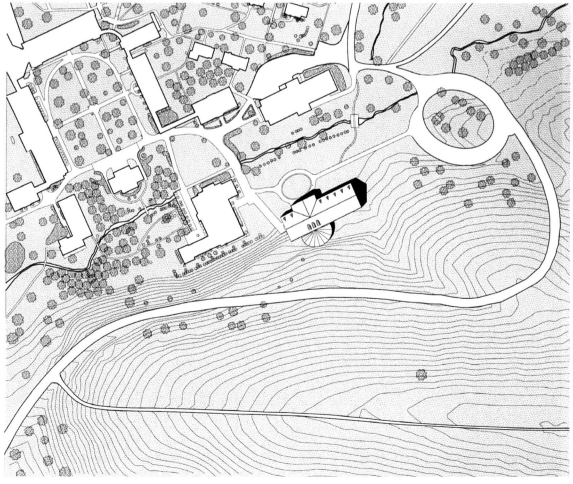

Campus site plan.

The library includes a Coffee Commons, which was requested by the Student Government Association, possibly because of the popularity of such features in large bookstore franchises. Although coffee is not to be brought into the library proper, the bar connects to the front porch, with its "Hollins Rockers," helping to make the library a comfortable place to read, discuss, and socialize.

In addition to ample individual seating, the building contains two large reading rooms, one on the first floor and another above it on the second. The first-floor reading room contains current periodicals and the one on the second floor contains folio (oversize) volumes. There are reading alcoves at each end of the floors as well as several group study rooms.

Archives and Special Collections are located next to the Hollins Authors Room. The architects designed space for researchers within Special Collections, but the space needs of the collection itself won out, resulting in no supervised space for researchers other than what can be borrowed from staff work areas. The Hollins Authors Room next door could provide such research space, were it not cut off visually from the Special Collections area itself.

In the basement are Media Services, including the media collection, office, circulation, multimedia suite, editing studio, television studio, and a large screening room with adjacent control room. The building also includes two art gallery nooks.

Auditorium/screening room.

Screening room from podium with projection room in background.

Basement Level

1. Auditorium/Screening Room
2. Audio/Visual Classroom
3. Mechanical
4. Television Studio
5. Viewing Booth
6. Compact Shelving

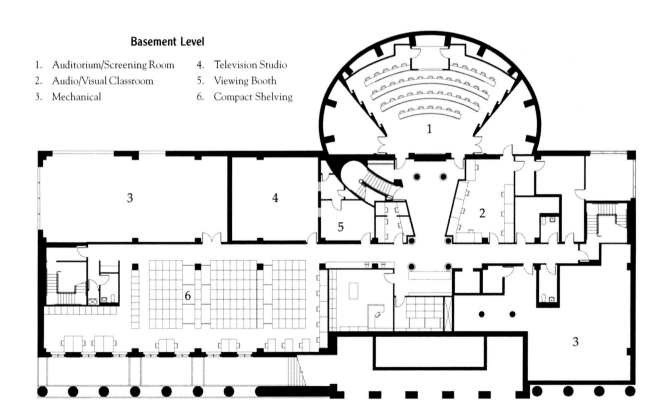

Coffee Commons.

Seating is a combination of study tables and lounge seating. Computers for the online public access catalog (OPAC) are provided throughout the building. A library instruction room uses laptops. There is also a computer nook that was not yet equipped in the summer of 1999. Media has general-purpose computers, televisions, and video-cassette recorders.

Part-way through the building program, the president, chief academic officer, and head librarian all departed. The new library director recalculated the shelf space in both the old and the new libraries. The previous administration had stated that the new building would hold more books than the old. In fact, it would hold less. At this point the university could have decided to expand the size of the building program or to reduce the size of other program elements in order to allow for more shelving in the new building. Instead, it decided to put lesser-used print materials into off-site storage, from which they could be retrieved with a day's notice. In so doing, Hollins joined the ranks of three other institutions included in this survey (Colorado State, Dickinson, and Marshall) in consigning lesser-used print materials to permanent storage, while building a new library with shelf space sufficient to house better-used materials and to allow for collection growth.

Both the circulation and the reference desks, located in the first-floor entrance lobby, are directly below the central stairs to the floors above and to their reading rooms. The university opted for an ash hardwood floor, rather than the carpeting suggested by the architects, in the entrance lobby. The combination of the acoustically-reflective flooring and the open stairway to the floors above has resulted in the transmission of sound from the two public service desks throughout the building—a serious problem especially for reference transactions, which should be confidential. The university has engaged an acoustical engineer in an effort to solve this problem and a similar noise problem in the Coffee Commons.

Circulation desk.

Opposite page:
3rd floor colonnade. Spiral
stair leading to reading loft.

Health Sciences and Human Services Library
University of Maryland-Baltimore

the architectural critic

Far from the image of the college campus as a protected, palatial setting—the classic American ideal of the academy on the edge of a woods—the University of Maryland-Baltimore campus is an urban dweller. It edges up next to one of the city's premier civic landmarks—Oriole Park at Camden Yards—and is a conglomeration of buildings old and new, historic and not-so-important. Into this gritty context, Perry Dean Rogers & Partners has placed a faithfully urban library, a building that hums with the life of the city and forges links with its neighbors.

The University of Maryland Health Sciences and Human Services Library occupies a full city block on the campus's eastern edge. This 190,000-square-foot building is a bulky, urban presence, a masculine object rendered in lasting materials of brick, limestone, and steel (the building's visual weight is reduced with the lavish use of the light-colored stone on its principal facades). These same materials are found in the library's context, and the new ties tightly to what is already there.

The library as seen from Davidge Hall.

One only needs to look at the surrounding neighborhood to understand the library's form. Its size and shape are similar to those around it. The long east wall along Greene Street cants slightly, pulling back as it moves north to the exclamatory tower at the corner. In this way the building not only serves as a gateway to the campus, but literally appears to swing open like a gate, and in so doing gives more prominence to the tower.

The tower itself is an assertive landmark, anchoring the building at the corner of Greene and Pratt Streets. It also marks the library's location on the campus skyline. A pinwheel of bollards arc back to the student union building next to the library (which connects to it) and defines an intimate plaza that the two buildings share. The tower and its tall canted window also denote the proximity of the medical school's most hallowed structure—Davidge Hall—built in 1807 and the oldest building in continuous use for medical education in the U.S.

On the west elevation is the library's tell tale "crab claw" which arcs out of the building to provide a loading dock on the first floor. It was so dubbed by the clients, who immediately recognized it as a part of one of the region's most popular seafood. Of course, context is everything. When the building was being designed in Boston, this element was routinely referred to as the "lobster claw."

Main lobby.

Main entrance on Pratt Street.

The library's plan is rationale yet full of surprises. The rectilinear frame on four of the six floors contains book stacks at its center, with a variety of seating at the periphery. The figural tower alternates as study space, lounge, classroom, and demonstration space. The crab claw houses administrative, computers, and other library services. The building's organization and plan, notes M.J. Tooey, associate library director, "is very traditional in nature, yet the infrastructure and use of the space allows for future flexibility."

At the very heart of the library is its most monumental space—a dramatic staircase that rises five stories in contiguous runs, so that one can stand at the bottom of the stairs and look straight up through the building's six stories. The staircase is a powerful, unifying device that stitches the multitude of library spaces together. It helps to orient the visitor who can easily move from one level to another. And it becomes an important social space, where people meet in moving through the library. Throughout, strong colors vibrate and enliven the interior, particularly a curving red wall at the entry that splays to reveal the grand flight of stairs and rises with it.

Those who work in and use the library most appreciate its light a color, and the plethora and variety of spaces devoted to study—either individually or in groups of assorted sizes. Such spaces are scattered throughout the library, some of them offering views out over the campus.

Stairway with reference to the left, and current periodicals readers overlooking the lobby from above.

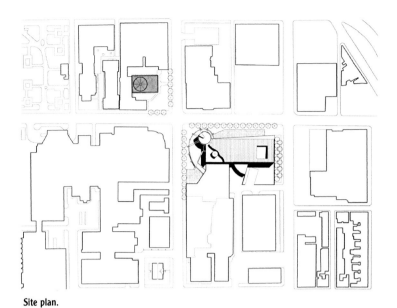

Site plan.

The Health Sciences and Human Services Library graciously meets its immediate aims—to provide a state-of-the-art facility for the pursuit of science. But it also fulfills a larger purpose, that of building the institution up and putting it on the map. In the words of university president David J. Ramsay, "Those who see our new library, from the outside and inside, will have to doubt as to the seriousness of our academic mission. This wonderful building puts us in a leadership position on an international scale."

Oriole Park from a group study window.

Reference and periodicals reading rooms and the tower cafe at night.

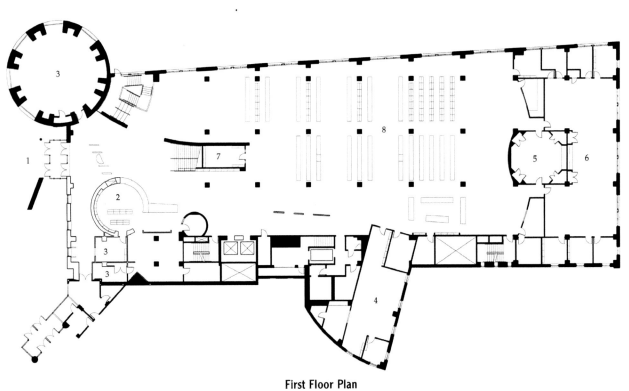

First Floor Plan

1. Main Entrance
2. Circulation Desk and Reserves
3. Tower Cafe
4. Computing and Technology Services
5. Conference Room
6. Information and Instructional Services
7. Copying
8. Reference

the academic librarian

The Health Sciences and Human Services Library at the University of Maryland-Baltimore (UM-B) is one of the most impressive of the group. Its entry atrium is striking from both inside and out. The exterior of its entry tower appears more distinctive in photographs than in situ, where it blends comfortably into the context of the University of Maryland Medical System building directly across the street. Similar materials were used in both buildings and the tower itself recalls the UMMS entry. But as soon as one steps inside the building, the sweep of line and color takes one's breath away. As in several other PDR&P libraries, there is a grand, double-height atrium entrance. But UM-B's colors are much stronger and bolder here. These colors are more visible from the outside at night when viewed through the large windows. Curvilinear walls contrast strongly with a grand staircase that rises from the entryway up five stories to the top floor. The only floor not reached by this stairway is the lower floor. As with Hollins, there is a coffee shop on the first floor, but separated from the library proper so that food and drink will not be brought into the building.

Detail of canted tower window.

The layout of the building is quite simple and repetitive from floor to floor. The building is a block long, but less than a block wide, making for a space that is deeper than it is wide. On all of the floors above the first, stacks form the core of the building with group study rooms on the block-long street side and staff offices on the other long side. The main floor repeats the pattern of staff offices on one side, but with the rest of the floor devoted to the reference collection, computers, and study tables. The lower floor is devoted entirely to computing and information technology spaces. The top floor houses administrative offices, Special Collections, and a spectacular Board Room. Color is used to define, separate, and make transitions. Striking floor lamps border and help to define the central staircase. The building connects internally to the Student Union next door.

The amount of space devoted to users on this urban commuter campus is far more than at any of the other libraries included in this survey. There are 900 seats, 1,600 data connections, and 42 study rooms, most with windows, for a student population of 5,700 headcount (about 2,000 full-time-equivalent), plus another 4,300 medical center employees. In the first year of operation, the new building has been used by nearly twice as many people as used the former library across the street: 447,556 compared to 235,512. Students, most of whom commute, need someplace to be when they are on campus, and the library is it. There are no residence halls, and limited space to "hang out" in other buildings. Of all the libraries visited, this one also has the most expansion room for library materials, housing all of the existing collection plus twenty years of expansion space.

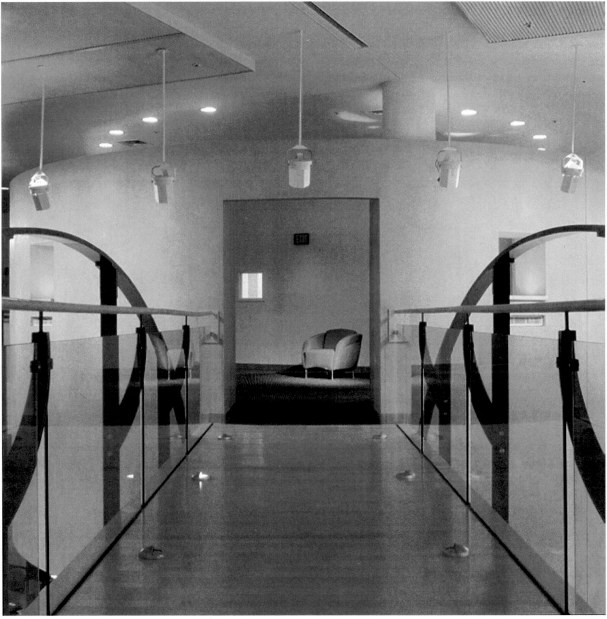

The lobby bridge.

A view of the stacks in relation to the stair.

With the exception of on-duty public-services staff, most staff are not easily accessible to the public. Most offices are located behind closed—and locked—doors in such a way that the public is probably unaware of them. UM-B is a graduate-level health sciences branch of a commuter university in a major city, and its staff do not need to have the same access to faculty and students as might be the case in a liberal arts college (see Dickinson below). The urban environment also means a heightened concern with security issues—UM-B's library has a guard at the entrance and a sign-in requirement, which none of the other six libraries had. The permanent library staff at UM-B is also several times larger than that at the liberal arts colleges because there are no resident undergraduates to be employed. As a result, the amount of space needed for permanent staff—and permanent staff offices—is several times greater.

The division of staff onto several floors in long, narrow bands of offices, however, makes for problems of communication. Access Services (circulation, reserves, electronic reserves, interlibrary loan, photocopy, and stacks management) is split on two floors (1 and 3) that are not contiguous. Likewise, Resources Management (acquisitions, serials, cataloging, historical, and special collections) is divided on three floors: 2, 4, and 5. The various computing services are awkwardly arranged for communication as well. Several staff complained that natural patterns of workflow are frustrated, rather than facilitated, by the building. Although everyone is happy not to be sitting on top of other people, staff must now go out of their way to see the people with whom they need to communicate. Several people commented that, while the public spaces are very flexible (essentially big, open rooms that can be rearranged as needed), staff spaces are far less so. Even when workstations can be moved, wiring cannot follow easily.

A large part of the reason for this less-than-ideal arrangement for staff has to do with the fact that staff spaces were planned for existing staff configurations and for some that were being planned when the building was first laid out. In one case, a key player was not yet on the staff, and when she did come, her space had already been planned in ways that could not be changed but that were not optimal from her perspective. A planned administrative reorganization that never took place resulted in some spaces that had to be reassigned at the last minute. State guidelines also limited the amount of space any employee could have based upon the person's level of employment, rather than based upon need. A lower-level employee in computing who needed a lot of space for equipment would not have been eligible for it, whereas an administrator with less need for space would have been entitled to a large office.

Hence, this is a building that works very well for its users, but somewhat less well for its staff. It has worked well also for the university. UM-B is an urban campus. It turns out more doctors who actually practice medicine in the state (as opposed to doing research or going elsewhere) than any other. But it has less visibility than the University of Maryland at College Park, and UM-B's medical school is less well-known than Johns Hopkins'. The neighborhood in which UM-B is located has been declining until recently, but the construction of two new sports stadiums at the nearby Camden Yards and the proximity of the Inner Harbor with its tourist attractions has begun to transform the area. The new library, with its daring and impressive architecture, has become a new anchor for the West Side empowerment zone, and has deliberately involved itself in community events, such as a Dr. Seuss birthday celebration for neighborhood children, a *Baltimore Sun* photograph exhibit, and an exhibit for the visually impaired. Several people commented that the new library has helped to recruit new faculty and students, and has even helped to recruit good library staff with no increase in pay.

A view from Pratt Street.

Main entrance.

Flo K. Gault Library for Independent Study
The College of Wooster

the architectural critic

The Flo K. Gault Library addition to Andrews Library at the College of Wooster in Ohio solves a number of problems simultaneously, while making a strong new link to the campus plan. At 30,000 square feet, the addition is a little over half the existing building's 56,000 square feet. Perry Dean Rogers & Partners' work also involved renovation of the older building to bring it into the 21st Century with the latest in computer technology, with access to all campus library databases, local area information networks, and the Internet.

The exterior form and materials of the Gault addition are examples of the architect's most sensitive and inventive uses of contextual design. Andrews Library, built in the 1960s, is limestone clad in an austere, stripped classical style. This symmetrical, three-story, rectangular building is longest along its north-south axis, with entrances on the east and west facades. To the west of Andrews is the campus center, a quadrangle dominated by Kauke Hall. To the north is Memorial Walk, a major pedestrian route that links many of the campus buildings.

The decision to add to Andrews on the north side makes sense for several reasons. There was open space for expansion, the addition could unite with Andrews without diluting the original building's form, and the new addition could tie into Memorial Walk, forging an important new link in the campus circulation. The architects created a new building that is the same height and width as Andrews. Gault is clad in the same limestone skin; copies cornices, molding, and other exterior details from Andrews; has fenestration on its east and west facades that

Detail at intersection of old and new.

echoes that of the older building; and is capped with a painted metal roof of the same design. The new building pulls away from Andrews and connects to it with a recessed glassy wall. The addition's southeast and southwest corners are rendered in glass block, which glows at night. A dramatic departure from Andrews is found on Gault's north wall, which addresses Memorial Walk. The limestone walls seem to pull apart, and between them rises a three-story faceted, curved glass wall that reveals Gault's interior. In front of this curtain of crystal is a glassy clock tower that hold's the library's new entrance, and a stair that curls from the second to third floor. This skillful extension takes its place along Memorial Walk with a generously scaled plaza as though it has always been a part of Wooster.

Opposite page:
Entrance plaza.

Previous page:
The new entrance on Memorial Walk

This liberal arts college is distinguished by its I.S.Program, which requires seniors to complete a written thesis for graduation. One of the goals for the new library was not only to accommodate students in their pursuit of independent study, but to express it as an important feature of the college. Gault and Andrews are now rife with independent study carrels, nearly 300 of them found on all four levels (including one below grade) and in a wonderful attic space that is the essence of a scholar's garret. Group study rooms are found on the main floor, with a foreign language learning lab and audiovisual materials on the ground floor. Most of the rest of Andrews and Gault is devoted to stacks and carrels, all of which are wired for computers. On the second and third levels, the carrels are pushed to the outside walls, while on the other levels they are often positioned next to sunny windows. The effect is stunning. At night, as one wanders past the library, the building is ablaze with light on all its levels, with students hard at work in their study carrels.

Independent study carrels overlooking the entry. Note the lockable storage.

The reference room, with portals to the original library to the left and right of the new stair.

As at the University of Maryland's new library in Baltimore, Gault is a treasure chest of natural light and vigorous color. A shaft of light fills a linchpin staircase that joins the new to the old. Librarian Damon Hickey reports that students respond strongly to the bright spaces and the surfaces of vigorous color in shades of yellow and red. Under the long gray skies of Ohio winters, he notes, "those warm colors lend a cheerfulness." Gault's arresting vistas of space, linking it to Andrews, further energize a library that draws students as a magnet. The attraction is potent: technology, color, light, and a special place of one's own for scholarly pursuits.

The free-standing glass wall highlights the independent study carrels.

the academic librarian

The College of Wooster's Flo K. Gault Library is an addition to its thirty-year-old Andrews Library. The library staff was interested primarily in additional seating and stack space in the new building. The administration, operating on the assumption that few people want to give major sums for an annex to a library with someone else's name on it, conceived of the project as a building with its own identity, its own name, and even its own entrance.

Every Wooster senior is required to complete a major two-semester project, most of which involves the writing and oral defense of a senior thesis. In preparation for this senior hurdle, juniors take one-semester Independent Study (I.S.) courses, which serve as introductions to the research methods in their disciplines. The I.S. requirement is unusual among American colleges, and is hard for many prospective students and their parents to grasp. The college administration decided that, instead of building a library annex, it would build a new library, attached to the old, and

A variety of carrel configurations.

feature the I.S. program in its architecture. Prominent in its design were 285 I.S. carrels for seniors, each with its own storage locker, study lamp, electrical power outlet, and data wiring. A clever use of split-level flooring enabled the architects to "stack" four levels of carrels into two floors of library, with still more carrels on the third floor, in a "crow's nest" devoted entirely to carrels, and even in Andrews Library. Many of these carrels are more visible from outside the building than from within, where they are hidden behind book stacks. The impression from the outside is of students in every window, busily engaged in their I.S. projects. The students themselves are able to look out on the campus, while simultaneously feeling secluded within. The administration's decision to emphasize I.S. seating in the new building meant that very little general seating was provided. At first this appeared to be a problem, until it became apparent that non-seniors felt free to use unoccupied carrels for study.

Since Andrews Library was classical and symmetrical in its plan, no attempt was made to change its proportions. Rather, the new building was attached to the north end, with a new grand entrance onto the campus's main pedestrian thoroughfare, Memorial Walk. The two buildings were separated visually by a recessed connector and glass-block windows that glow like faceted jewels at night. Since Andrews Library had two entrances (east and west) already, the new entrance gave the combined buildings three, requiring two service points. Despite the concern of librarians that such an arrangement would require additional student staffing, the administrative decision to build a "new" library, rather than one that would be viewed simply as an extension of the old, and the geography of the campus effectively dictated the outcome. Making virtue out of necessity, the librarians designated one of the service points for reserve materials and the other for interlibrary loan, with both serving also for general circulation of library materials.

The addition's massing reflects that of the original building.

Other compromises were made. The elongation of the reference area, stretching from the new north entrance of Gault Library half-way into Andrews Library meant that no location for the reference desk could be ideal. The decision to place it in Gault Library, as near as possible to Andrews Library, still separated it visually and put it too far away from the computer workstations where students usually need help. Also, the ways in which the two buildings came together precluded a continuous arrangement of the collection in call-number order across both buildings and from the top floor to the bottom. Instead, coherent pieces of the collection were fitted into appropriate spaces, sometimes without regard to the overall sequencing of the collection.

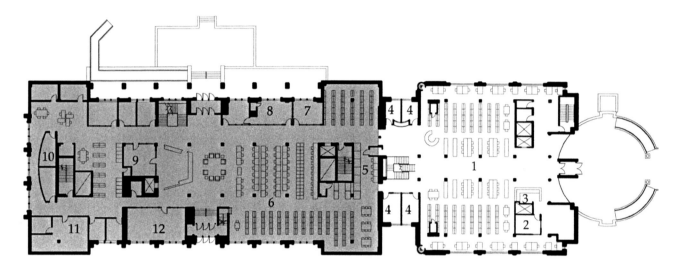

Main Level

1. Reference Collection
2. Circulation Supervisor
3. Reserves
4. Group Study
5. Maps
6. Document Reference
7. Lister Room
8. Library Administrative Offices
9. Interlibrary Loan
10. Government Information Librarian
11. Government Information
12. Andrews Room

The peculiarity of Wooster's library program dictated the location of public service offices. Since all librarians took turns staffing the reference desk, with no one librarian's having overall responsibility for reference, and since no librarian wanted to be seen as "the reference librarian," no librarian's office was located close to the reference desk. If this staffing pattern should change, the physical arrangement of offices could prove inconvenient.

Recognizing the growing trend toward collaborative learning, the new building included four group study rooms, and a fifth was carved out of space in Andrews Library. Experience has shown that ten would be well-used sometimes.

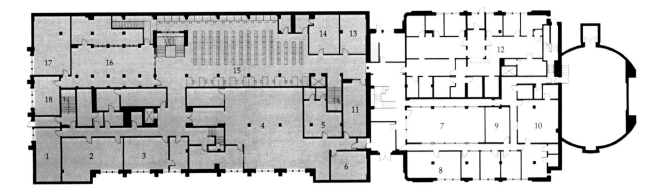

Lower Level

1. Staff Lounge
2. Davis Room
3. Writing Center
4. Technical Services
5. Bindery Preparation
6. Gift Books
7. McCreight Learning Laboratory
8. Audio/Visual
9. Graphics Room
10. Audio/Visual Technical Area
11. Mail Room
12. Registrar & Financial Aid
13. Nesbitt Room
14. Bechtel Room
15. Oversize General Collection
16. Special Collections
17. Notestein Room
18. Special Collections Librarian

Internal shifts were effected in order to create in Andrews Library a new Special Collections area. Formerly, special collections had been shelved in multiple rooms and locked cases throughout the building, making it impossible to consolidate them or to provide service for library users. The consolidation of special collections accompanied a shift of staff resources to provide daily coverage. The new space provides an elegant reading room with exhibit space, a workroom for staff, and a closed-stack area on a lower floor, filled with mobile compact shelving and accessible to staff only.

When the library staff began its planning, the impact of library computing was only beginning to become apparent. By the time the library was under construction, it was increasingly obvious that computing would dominate library development for the foreseeable future. The addition and renovation reflected this revolution, but incompletely. All 285 new study carrels were wired for both electrical power and data. Data was supplied to almost every room and office, as well as to locations where public computer workstations would be placed. But neither electrical power nor data wiring was supplied to study tables, lounge seating, or the old carrels. As requested by the library staff, several classrooms were included in Andrews Library and the addition, primarily for library instruction. But none of these rooms was wired to be fully electronic, with computer projection or workstations for each student—a deficiency that would limit their usefulness for library instruction. The relative newness of electronics to libraries meant also that the cost of data wiring was overlooked in the preparation of the budget, as a result of which the project went over budget.

Some consideration was given to moving Academic Computing Services into Gault Library, but such a move would have required construction of an additional floor, without providing even as much room as Computing had already in another building. The physical separation of Computing from Libraries meant that a future organizational merger of the two units would be either less likely or more difficult.

Stylistically, the Flo K. Gault Library for I.S. strongly resembles Andrews Library in its style, building materials, and fenestration. The major departure is the dramatic new north entrance, a two-part, three-story curtain-glass wall supported only by a system of trusses that distribute the load of the glass and the force of air against it into the building itself. The two curtain walls are separated by an impressive glass-and-limestone clock tower. At night, interior lights and spotlights (both interior and exterior) play off the limestone walls to create an impression, clearly visible from the city street, that is both dramatic and welcoming. Electronic Westminster chimes broadcast from large, concealed speakers toll the hours. Interior design, especially in Gault Library, is simultaneously brighter and more colorful than in Andrews. Whereas Andrews Library made heavy use of oak, a medium-dark wood, Gault uses light-colored maple paneling and carrels, with darker cherry for chairs, tables, and trim. New stacks are white, in contrast to the several pastel colors in Andrews Library. Skylights bring more natural light into Gault Library, and warm reds and yellows are used on some walls and ceilings as a counterbalance to the cooler blues and grays of northern Ohio's long winters.

The reference desk.

Waidner Library
Dickinson College

the architectural critic

The Waidner Library addition at Dickinson College in Carlise, Pennsylvania, is an interesting contrast to Perry Dean Rogers & Partners' work at Gault Library, where the architects extruded a new addition from an existing building. At Dickinson, the approach is to radically depart from the existing Spahr Library, and return to the architecture of much older buildings on campus for inspiration.

Main entrance with battered stone wall beyond.

The design challenge at Dickinson was formidable. How to add to a building that seems to have been designed to spurn additions—a self-contained lock-box of books that was inwardly focused and architecturally aloof. Spahr's pedigree was pure 1960s. There are libraries just like it on campuses around the country (one immediately thinks of Skidmore, Ownings & Merrill's Beinecke Rare Book Library at Yale, a pristine, rectangular container of alabaster walls).

Unlike Beinecke, Spahr was not worth replicating in any way. Its heavy, concrete frame and walls of infill limestone are scaleless and unfriendly. One of the first strategies proposed by Perry Dean Rogers & Partners was to wrap Spahr in a new skin and create an addition around it (an approach akin to what the architects had done at Olin Library at Wesleyan University) but that idea was rejected by the client. The architect then wisely chose to locate the new addition just west of Spahr, where it could forge a connection to the campus.

The 46,000-square-foot addition links into the existing library on the 72,000-square-foot building's west side with a glazed connection that clearly separates old from new. However, these glassy walls replicate Spahr's tripartite horizontal window division—a subtle, harmonic reference. The addition is the same width as Spahr. In plan, it's as if a section of the older library has been sliced off and pulled away, and the void infilled with the glazed connector (on the south side, the connector wall steps back to allow room for an old Sycamore tree).

Opposite page:
Elliptical reading room
overlooking Dickinson walk.

But from there, Waidner goes its own way, absorbing from the older campus buildings (some of which date from the Civil War, and earlier) its distinctive forms and sympathetic materials. The bulbous shape of a new reading room to the north, a slightly canted wall along which group study spaces are found, and the gracefully curved glazed connector wall all serve to soften the harshness of Spahr. In and around these soft shapes and angles is a new terraced garden that connects to Dickinson Walk (a pedestrian way that links the building to dorms and the student union) and also delivers light to lower level library spaces.

The exterior of Waidner is welcoming and familiar. Its grand, flat-roofed entry canopy supported by a small grove of spindly columns reaches out to the campus like a handshake. This element has the uncanny feel of 1960s Late Modernism (Edward Durrell Stone, anyone?) but the scale is in check and appropriate for the context. It is a great entrance, like opening night at the opera, that gives the library a necessary formal bearing. The addition's walls are of rough-cut ashlar limestone taken from the same quarry used for Dickinson's Old West building, designed by Benjamin Henry Latrobe (a noted architect in the late 18th- early 19th-Century, who also designed interiors of the U.S. Capitol). The material has a warm, rich texture that links the new library to the fabric of Dickinson's campus.

The thick, battered stone wall contains window seats; double-height bay window overlooks landscape.

Cuts in battered wall provide window seats and reflect light to the interior.

Inside, Perry Dean Rogers & Partners created a light and friendly interior that immediately makes you feel at home. Like many of the firm's libraries, this one has the feel of a large home, with domestic touches like built-in window seats and a fireplace for convivial gatherings on the upper level of "the nest," an intimate student lounge over the first-floor circulation desk that juts out into the two-story connector space. From the vantage of the nest, one can look back through the space and out the curved window wall at Waidner's rustic limestone walls. Scattered throughout the building (including the renovated Spahr building, which is now devoted almost solely to stack space) are comfortable areas were study groups can meet and work, with portals for computer connections.

These new group studies areas, notes library department chair Kris Senecal, are one of the most welcome and popular features in the new building. A library design attentive to the needs of students and staff, which then considers the larger world of the campus, is not lost on its users. "The combination of building materials, such as natural maple and limestone, and the blending of traditional and modern elements really makes this work as a public building," Senecal says, "and I think they will stand the test of time."

The reference desk is centrally located and easily seen from the main entry and reference collections.

the academic librarian

The goal for Waidner Library at Dickinson College in Carlisle, Pennsylvania, was to make the library more inviting and to provide growth space. The Spahr Library, to which Waidner is attached, was built in 1966. Linoleum was used liberally, even in the study carrels, along with aluminum and stone. Furniture was hard and uncomfortable. The college had subsequently purchased beanbag chairs just in order to have some soft seating. The new building adds group studies, electronics, and increased reader space. The renovation of Spahr Library, which took place at the same time as the construction of Waidner, made it more useful and blended it with the new building. The old furniture was replaced completely.

Libraries and Computing are separate departments at Dickinson. The libraries include eighty computers, more than any other department except math-science. They also have their own electronic services librarian, plus a part-time person from Academic Computing, who has an office in the library. But as at Wooster, Computing is not housed in the library building.

The expansion of the Spahr Library at Dickinson College resembles in many ways the expansion of the Andrews Library at the College of Wooster, an institution that is also similar in size and program. In both projects an existing library building was serviceable but inadequate to hold an expanding collection and to provide new technology. In both

Oval reading room as seen from Dickinson Walk.

cases the new building was given its own name and its own visual distinction, while linking comfortably, both inside and out, with the existing library.

But the differences between the two projects are as striking as their similarities, reflecting in part the differences in the library programs. At Dickinson all of the librarians provide reference services and act as liaisons with academic departments, coordinating collection development and providing library instruction for them, as they do also at Wooster. But at Dickinson, which has a larger staff, librarians also catalog books, take turns teaching First-Year Seminars (including advising the students in the section for their first two years of college), and rotate as chair of the libraries. There has been, in other words, no director of libraries. Those librarians who are not teaching First-Year Seminars divide up the responsibility for being liaisons with faculty members who are teaching other sections.

Main entry with colored connector at right.

This sharing of multiple tasks by all librarians meant that library offices needed to be located in such a way as to allow them easy access to faculty, staff, and technical services staff. And so, rather than locate library offices against an exterior wall with a window for each, the librarians opted to place their offices in the center of the floor, with the reference collection (public service area) on one side and technical services on the other. Each office has two doors, permitting its occupant easy access in either direction. Unfortunately, walls do not rise to the ceiling, meaning that private conversations can be overheard by other librarians, technical services staff, and patrons.

Despite an impressive multi-story atrium that serves as the entrance lobby, noise transmission is not a problem, except for the librarians in their offices. Students are generally aware of which areas of the buildings will be quiet, and which will be conversational. One librarian commented that the building is spacious, airy, and very impressive. Another lauded the beautiful, good study spaces and classrooms; the good meshing of old and new buildings; the "grand hotel" effect of the lobby; and the popularity of the building with students.

Entry Level

1. Group Study
2. Lounge
3. Reading Room
4. Carrels
5. Tech Services
6. Information
7. Book Stack
8. Open Study Area
9. Reference
10. Circulation
11. Computer Lab

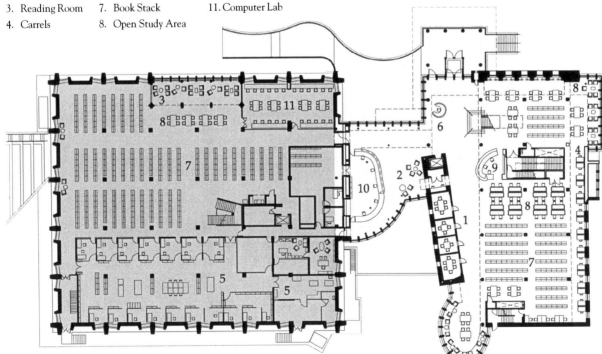

View from study lounge above circulation desk looking toward main entrance.

Opposite page:
Main entrance from ramp.

The main lobby includes a clock wall with clocks that show the time in various places where Dickinson has study abroad. There is a fireplace in one study space. There are several areas with large windows and easy chairs where there is lots of light, especially on overcast days, with striking views of trees and mountains. In addition to general seating there are many unassigned study carrels with adjustable light fixtures. All carrels in the new building have been wired. The buildings are bright, with white walls and maple woodwork (found in all the libraries visited). New maple end panels on the old stacks, maple wainscoting in the old building, and new carpet throughout tie the buildings together. Old, dark columns were sheathed in white sheet rock to add light and to make the old building uniform with the new. The same new maple furniture was used in both buildings. In contrast to many other PDR&P libraries, the use of color is sparing. The only accent color is a very pale mauve.

Study lounge over entrance looking out through canopy.

Special Collections Reading Area.

One of the most striking features of the libraries is the special collections room, which is large and beautiful with lots of well-lit research and exhibit space. This area contains Joseph Priestley's library and some of his laboratory equipment and other antique scientific apparatus.

Complaints about the building have been relatively few and minor. The combination of audiovisual materials and reserves into a single area of the building has not been as successful as hoped, but the problem (if it is one) can be remedied fairly easily. Indeed, one of the striking features of this building is that it makes very few compromises to larger institutional considerations and is, for better or worse, a librarian's building. If the program of the library were to change—if, for example, the library staff became more specialized and departmental than it is now—the present location of the librarians' offices in a line separating Technical Services from a public area might be less functional. The college also decided to make permanent the off-site storage of some 100,000 lesser-used volumes, despite the hopes of some faculty and staff that all would be made readily available in the new library.

Morgan Library
Colorado State University

the architectural critic

One of the "Shalt Nots" of library design is: Thou Shalt Not Design an L-Shaped Library. This plan form results in dead-ends and inefficient circulation. Colorado State University in Fort Collins was cursed with just such a building, whose puny entrance at the crux of the L was difficult to find and functioned poorly. Added to this was a large plaza in front of the library that did not relate to it. The challenge at Morgan Library was to redress these deficiencies, expand the building by 109,000 square feet, and create a landmark at the heart of the campus.

Morgan Library is a building that captures all the light and color of the Colorado locale and blends in the latest in electronic technology. The new addition is a complex melange of organic forms and spatial explosions that overtakes the original building and remakes it totally. The new seems to attach itself to the old starting in the plaza. It then backs into the shell of the existing structure like a hermit crab, and then blossoms out to the west with a sweeping wall of glass that takes in the whole of the Front Range of the Rocky Mountains. The addition funnels and focuses, its tall, stony entry wall asserting itself like a billboard or radar disk that

The entrance from the northeast.

draws you in. Walls then splay and redirect visitors, propelling them in the direction of the mountain view. Here is found a generous reading room that is penetrated by a vertical shaft of color and light. At the top floor, up pops a periscope overlooking the range.

The exterior colors and materials tie the building to the Colorado landscape. The entry wall, which faces a newly designed plaza, moves out from the building and gives the library a scale appropriate to this outdoor space. The curved plane is rendered in yellow and ochre sandstone, which is quarried locally and captures the color of the mountains. The north-facing wall is curved just enough to capture a bit of sun, which makes the rough texture of the stone sing. On the building's west elevation, the same stone is used, but its texture is rendered less aggressively by virtue of its flat, uncurved surface. The other predominant material is synthetic stucco in a warm buff, which contrasts well with the stone.

The west elevation with view of mountains.

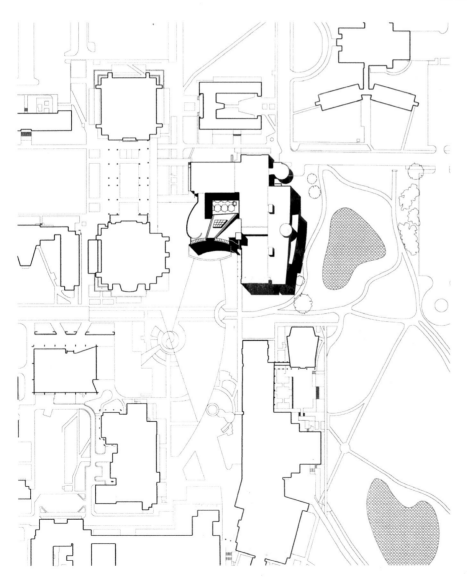

Site plan.

View of western reading room.

One of the potential pitfalls in adding to this L-shaped building was ending up with a plan that would be confusing and difficult to navigate. The architects solved this problem with natural light and the Colorado "Big Sky" as elements to help orient visitors, and a grand two-story space that makes visual connections between the building's four levels. The important role of daylight is apparent from the moment you step into Morgan. From the generous reception area and the "café" of tables and chairs that invite students to sit, linger, talk, or study, one can look out into a central courtyard that the architects created between the addition and the old building. Look straight up, and you are in a three-story shaft of space around which are found study areas and lounges. If you move to the west toward the circulation and information desks, you can see the Rockies in the distance through the three-story glass wall that constantly offers the mountains as a reference point. From these reference points—the courtyard, the mountains, and the multi storied spaces inside—the library's collection can be explored. And since the building is fully wired for computer access to its own collection and the Internet, your exploration can go further afield. There are reading rooms and pockets of space populated with tables for individual study or working groups at every level of the building. Some of them are right next to the windows with the sweeping views, while others are squirreled away down on the subterranean ground floor, away from all possible distractions.

The Colorado State University wanted a library that would provide a focal point for the campus, a building that would be a landmark. Morgan now serves that role. Students regularly stand for their graduation pictures in front of its curved entry wall—a backdrop that immediately identifies their alma mater. While the strong colors in the building have drawn mixed reactions, "You either love them or hate them," according to Reference Librarian Halcyon Enssle, the imaginative use of natural light and color make the library "an extremely positive place to work in," she says. And its influence has been felt beyond the campus. The university has been mounting art exhibits in the library, and inviting artists to lecture on their work. These events have not only drawn the campus community, but many from Fort Collins as well.

Western reading room overlooking the front range of the Rocky Mountains.

the academic librarian

Morgan Library at Colorado State University in Fort Collins suffered a major disaster before it opened officially. In 1997, one week after a new dean of libraries had taken up residence, a freak rainstorm crossed the Colorado Rockies and sat over the university, dropping 11 1/2 inches of rain in one afternoon. Water rose 8 1/2 feet outside the west wall of the new building, until the wall finally gave way. Stacks on the lower level, filled with bound periodicals, collapsed domino-like as the water rushed in. As a result, the library was not complete until January 1999. A new retaining wall has now been erected to the west of the building, should such a storm ever recur.

"Morgan Library" was the original name of the building before construction began, and the new Morgan Library is the old L-shaped Morgan Library with a new building wrapped around it. Even the original entrance is intact and visible across a central courtyard. The unroofed courtyard was designed as a quiet, quasi-outdoor study area, but has not proved popular because it is too hot in the summer and too cold in the winter. The courtyard creates a building with a square hole in the center, around which everything revolves. The third level is not connected all the way around. The building is full of light, with windows looking out either onto the courtyard or to the outside of the building. The

Interior courtyard.

architects intended that library users would orient themselves by reference to these vistas—angle of the courtyard, main plaza, mountains, and so on. But I found the building much harder to "read" than any other in this group. Even with a floor plan, it takes awhile to orient oneself. Some of the faculty and library staff would have preferred a "book box" addition to the older building to eliminate the L shape by making it into an enclosed square, sacrificing the courtyard for more growth space and an easier-to-read layout.

Social space/reading area inside front entrance.

Western elevation.

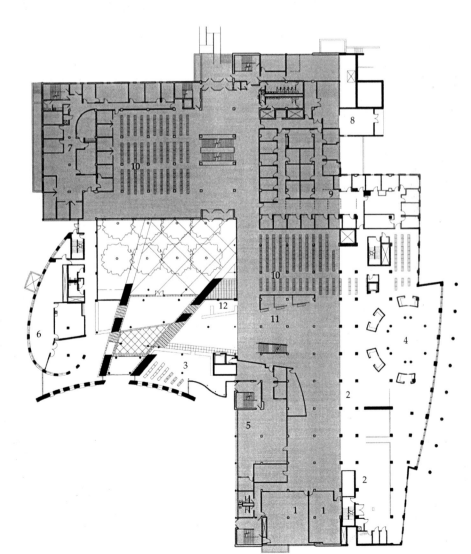

First Floor Plan

1. Electronic Classroom
2. Electronic Information Center
3. Circulation Desk
4. Reading Room
5. Access Service
6. Interlibrary Loan
7. Administration/Accounting
8. Shipping & Receiving
9. Cataloguing
10. Reference Collection
11. Reference Desk
12. Information Desk

Detail of windows framing the horizon.

Nevertheless, the new building is quite striking. Like Marshall, Dickinson, and UM-B, it boasts a grand multi-story atrium/lobby at its entrance, with striking use of color. The exterior echoes the use of red sandstone, tan sandstone, and tan poured concrete used elsewhere on campus. The strong use of "Van Gogh" colors and a dramatic third-floor sculpture inside create an uplifting feeling. Initially the university resisted the idea of expanding into the university's main plaza, which had been built to the exact dimensions of the Piazza of San Marco in Venice. And the profile of the original Morgan library had been kept deliberately low in order not to obstruct the view of the mountains beyond. But the dramatic new entrance seems a more fitting completion of the plaza, and the views of the mountains are still there—from the new reading rooms in the library, not from the plaza.

The building contains 11 group study rooms, 1.5 million "volumes" (of all formats), employs about 115 library staff, and serves a student body of some 22,500 full-time-equivalents, mostly residential. About 20 percent of the collection was removed following the flood, and it was not known how much would be salvaged. In addition, the university placed lesser-used parts of the collection in remote storage elsewhere on campus before construction began, with the intention that they would remain there indefinitely.

Previous page:
North facing front entrance.

An exhibit area just inside the main entrance is more noticeable from outside the building than from within. A skylit bridge on the second floor crosses under a large, dramatic, hanging sculpture. At night the reading windows, surmounted by a lighted cupola, glow. There is ample and varied seating throughout the building, including carrels, study tables, reading rooms, and lounge seating. The view of the Rocky Mountains, from the large reading rooms, is truly spectacular. There are, of course, computers throughout the building, as well as an assistive technology area for people with various disabilities.

Despite the confusion the shape of the enlarged building creates, it has been largely popular with both staff and students, who have used it in large numbers. Essentially this is an all-library library, with the exception of e-mail labs and a Center for Teaching and Learning, staffed by a faculty development consultant, that were added after the building program was drawn up. Computing resides elsewhere and is administratively separate.

The western elevation at dusk.

Third level reading area facing interior courtyard.

Timken Science Library
The College of Wooster

the architectural critic

The new Timken Science Library at The College of Wooster is actually in the oldest building on campus. Housing new within old became a theme in the design, where entirely new features such as a staircase and shelving are expressed in a crisp, modernist esthetic, while the building's classical elements such as columns and cornices are restored flawlessly.

Evolution and change are actually a constant in Timken's history. The library, as it was dedicated in 1900, was the gift of industrialist Henry Clay Frick (the only library he ever endowed) in memory of his parents, who had lived in Wooster. The building, which was the college's first free-standing library, was built in stages: first its west wing and a low stack wing to the north, then its east wing and another stack wing. Eventually a second story of stack space was added. The main entrance always faced west, toward University Street, and was at the top of a grand staircase that delivered visitors to a grandly appointed, two-story reading room. At its dedication, the limestone and granite building was hailed as a triumph of fire-proof construction. A year after it opened, the building that had previously housed Wooster's 22,000-volume library, Old Main, burned to the ground.

The principal façade. Note the entrance, now at grade, which was originally the main floor above.

The building served as the library for 62 years until the completion of Andrews Library on a nearby site to the east. It was then converted into a makeshift gallery and offices. With the expansion of Andrews with the new Flo K. Gault Library, it was pressed back into service as a library in which the college's scattered collection in the natural sciences could reside. Perry Dean Rogers & Partners' changes and additions to the building, now rededicated as the Timken Science Library in Frick Hall, reflect the architects' able skill in breathing new life into old buildings.

The science collection is some 35,000 volumes, and the original building's structure was never intended to support compact shelving. The solution was to essentially gut the stack wing to the north and build a new structure inside it, fitting three levels in all. Compact shelves are found on the lowest level. When the building was first constructed, most of the college buildings were to the south of it. Since then, the campus has expanded north, and most students and faculty approach Timken from this side. The architects created a new entrance on what had been the building's back-side, using limestone, metal, and glass detailed to recall the architecture of Andrews Library, not far away. Thus the new building makes a connection to it context, while expressing this new entrance as an obvious recent addition. The north entry hall is a wonderful, spirited, compressed space, with an energetic stair that leaps to the second and third levels with a steel framework sheathed in glass—it almost dematerializes.

Site Plan

1. Flo K. Gault Library
2. Timken Science Library

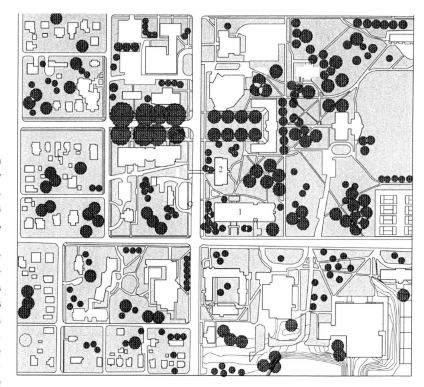

On the lowest level, accessible from either the north or south entry, is the new circulation desk rendered in light wood. This floor also contains administration areas, a computer lab, study rooms, storage, and other support space.

The jewel of the Timken Science Library is the main reading room on the main floor, with its faux marble columns and elaborate architrave with the names of some of the luminaries of the Western canon: Kant, Milton, Shakespeare, Newton, even Moses. Stretching from one end of the building to the other, the two-story reading room was restored according to an old color post card of the interior found by the science librarian and given to the architect. The card was posted in the design studio as a reminder of what the room could be. The result is the most dramatic space on campus. "People are awestruck by how beautiful it is," says librarian, Damon Hickey, especially the old alums for whom Timken is the only library at Wooster that they ever knew. "One visiting alumnus told me, 'It was never this good'," says Hickey. Four columns were added to the central colonnade, one of which conceals HVAC ducts, while equipment is hidden behind new portions of the architrave.

Ground Floor Plan

1. Vestibule
2. Lobby
3. Circulation Desk
4. Compact Shelving
5. Study Room
6. Office
7. Workroom
8. Computer Lab
9. Copier Room
10. Mechanical Room

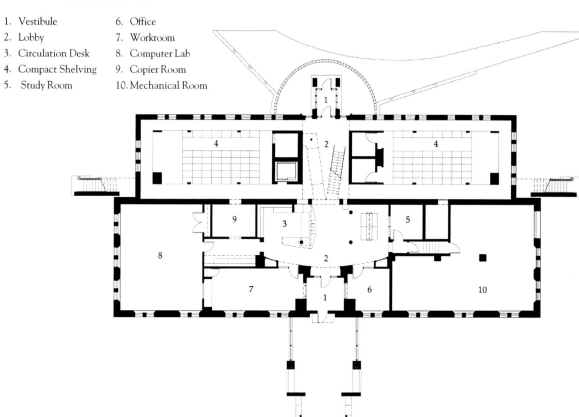

The computer workstations occupy the former vestibule. The columns to the right are original; the pair to the left are new, and house ductwork bringing air to the ceiling diffusers.

The old main entry into this space has been turned into a window overlooking the south entrance. At the west and east end of the room are free-standing mezzanines that have study carrels up top and periodicals below. These structures are rendered in clean, crisp materials that identify them as new additions, and they link to the third floor stack level. "They are a brilliant use of space," says Hickey, that offer new vantages of the reading room, and the students covet them.

Mezzanine Floor Plan

1. Carrel Mezzanine   3. Study Room
2. General Collection   4. Bridge

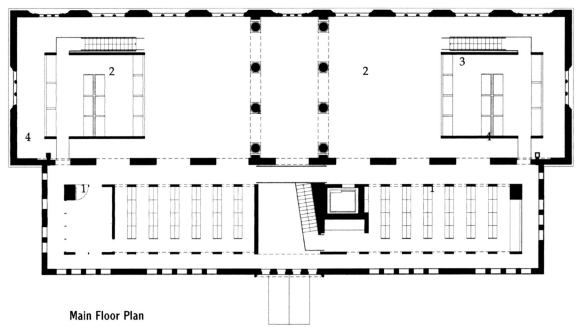

Main Floor Plan

1. Main Reading Room   4. General Collection
2. Reference Collection   5. Librarian's Office
3. Periodicals

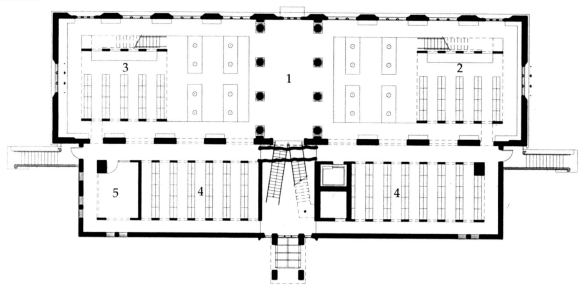

New entrance to the north.

the academic librarian

Opened in 1900, The College of Wooster's Frick Hall was built as a grand nineteenth-century library, with a double-height neoclassical reading room in front and stacks behind. The exterior, in limestone, mirrored the interior in style and decoration. The interior frieze included over each bay the names of great men of western civilization (prior to 1900), while the exterior frieze bore the names of academic disciplines. The reading room was originally suffused with color. A central bay was defined by full-height columns of the Corinthian order.

New accessible entrance.

In 1962, with the opening of Andrews Library, Frick Hall was minimally altered to house the college's art museum and various faculty and administrative offices. In the 1990s the college decided to move these elements elsewhere, creating the possibility of restoring the building as a library once again, to bring together the science collections that were housed in four buildings, three of which were unstaffed departmental libraries.

From the standpoint of library service, having the science collections in the same building as the non-science collections would have been desirable, but there were other issues involved. First, the science faculty wanted its own library, and was reluctant to give up departmental libraries otherwise. The science faculty and other college officials also saw the potential of a separate science library for recruiting outstanding science students and faculty. Second, the college had an interest in restoring as a library a building that had served that purpose for more than sixty years. The college considered connecting the two buildings, but rejected the idea as impractical (the floor levels of the two buildings were not the same) and too costly.

Opposite page:
The main reading room, with the inserted
mezzanine visible on the right.

Originally Frick Hall had only one, second-level entrance directly into the reading room. The renovated building, it was decided, would have two entrances, both at ground level to facilitate access by wheeled vehicles. The two entrances echoed the double-sided entrances to Andrews Library and several other campus buildings, while providing access both to the science buildings on one side and to Andrews Library on the other. Because of mechanical and other issues, the entire stack wing of the building had to be gutted and replaced by new floors at slightly different heights from the old ones. The limited size of the building also dictated the placement of mezzanines at each end of the main reading room, a brilliant move by the architects that consolidated current periodicals at one end and reference materials at the other, with carrel seating above each that provides new vistas of the reading room. These mezzanines were connected physically and through the use of colors and building materials to the new stacks. To provide adequate room for bound periodicals, compact shelving was used on the lower stack floor, and upper floors were constructed to withstand the weight of compact shelving, should it be needed later.

The limitations of the old building were felt in other ways as well. The back of the building had to be transformed from the plain back of a book-storage wing into an inviting library façade. Again the architects made virtue out of necessity by constructing a two-story entrance with straight lines, rectilinear columns, and glass-and-aluminum building materials that echoed those used in Andrews Library's west façade next door, thereby providing a visual unity to this library corner of the campus. Modern lighting, data wiring, a ground-floor computer laboratory, and HVAC duct work for air conditioning had to be inserted into a building not designed for them. (One duct problem was solved by creating two new, hollow Corinthian columns in the reading room that double as ducts.)

The resulting structure has been an unequivocal campus hit. The reading room is once again a campus treasure that inspires a sense of awe and quiet. With the replacement of the old entrance by a window, the addition of two new columns and pilasters, a thorough cleaning and repair of the dark oak woodwork and plaster, the construction of new bookcases, and the restoration of intense colors to the walls and frieze, the room has become once again the focal point of the building. One older alumnus commented, comparing it to its earlier life as a library, "It was never this good. This is not a renovation; it is an enhancement!" New technologies fit comfortably into the old building, making it an interesting blend of library designs spanning a century.

The north entrance.

Staircase details.

John Deaver Drinko Library
Marshall University

the architectural critic

If there is one building in this collection of libraries by Perry Dean Rogers & Partners that captures the future of library design—from a technological point of view—it is the John Deaver Drinko Library at Marshall University in Huntington, West Virginia. Since its completion, the university has hailed this building as "a cutting edge, 21st century facility," with 26 networked single and group study rooms, many of them with computers; three large collaboration rooms with teleconferencing capabilities; data ports in the lounge for patrons' laptop computers; a 25-

The west façade.

seat electronic training room; a 30-seat specialized electronic presentation room with two-way video capabilities; a 50-seat auditorium with notebook computers and two-way video and presentation capabilities; two conference rooms with network and multimedia capabilities; electronic document delivery to and from most locations in the library; and a multimedia library system that is web accessible. Patrons can also borrow laptop computers from the library and plug into one of 200 ports around the building for laptops (the entire building has some 800 computer ports).

Drinko is not only the university library. The building also contains computing services, telecommunications, instructional technology, and information technology for the entire campus. Given the building's position on the front line of the digital revolution, one might think that the book was on its way out, at least at this library. But Drinko was built with shelf capacity for over 200,000 volumes. Its design neatly expresses the current moment, when books of paper are giving way to books of bytes.

Drinko Library is located just south of Old Main, the most venerable building on campus. Old Main has the look of a castle, with its sturdy red brick walls, rusticated stone base and banding, and a central tower with four crenelated turrets. The client wanted the library to reflect this campus landmark, and Drinko has substantial walls of red brick with a light stone banding. On its west facade two solid shafts rise to suggest the towers of Old Main. At the bottom of this central element is a terra cotta archway salvaged from a building that once stood on the spot. Now surrounded by a base of rusticated stone, similar to that on Old Main, the archway somewhat perversely signals an entrance to Drinko, but this isn't the case. Although this west side is the library's major "public" face, as it addresses the campus and the town, its main entrance is actually to the east, off a network of pedestrian paths.

The main entrance.

The Computer Center.

Red brick facades extend south and north, bending around with a graceful curve to stop abruptly at a large, five-story glass cylinder—the building's tallest element. This linchpin of activity, through which one can see the buzz of several staircases and a reading room, marks Drinko's main entrance, where the library's "old" and "new" personalities merge. To the south of this cylinder a Corbusian facade of glass and stucco appears, behind which is a welcoming café on the first floor, with a reading room and administrative offices above. A stainless steel canopy arcs along a pedestrian path and connects back into the entry cylinder with a wavy tongue that passes through the glass walls and hovers over the circulation desk.

The lobby, with circulation desk.

The upper rotunda. Color identifies building systems and architectural forms.

Inside, Drinko's spaces are arranged with a logic that places people near windows and open vistas, while the collection and computer spaces reside at the building's heart. The glassy rotunda serves as an important orienting device in this large building, with stairways clinging to or flying through it. Here also is the architect's trademark use of color—strong primary shades that pop the eye and distinguish overlapping planes. In quieter spaces, such as the palatial 24-hour reading room on the first floor, the colors, textures, patterns, and materials are appropriately muted.

First Floor Plan

1. Entry
2. 24 Hour Reading Room
3. Cafe
4. Reference Collection
5. Special Collection
6. Circulation Workroom
7. Copy Center
8. Consultation
9. Office
10. Accounting & Operations
11. Public Services
12. Mail Room
13. Hardware
14. Shipping & Receiving
15. Mechanical/Electrical

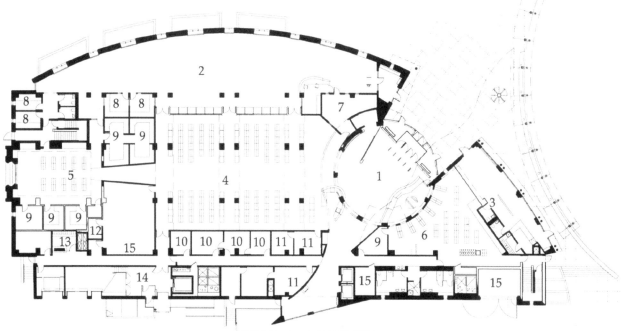

Second Floor Plan

1. Copy Center
2. Office
3. Mechanical/Electrical
4. General Collection
5. Periodicals
6. Media & Public Services
7. Group Study
8. Study
9. Readers
10. Reading Room
11. Carrels
12. Staff Lounge Area

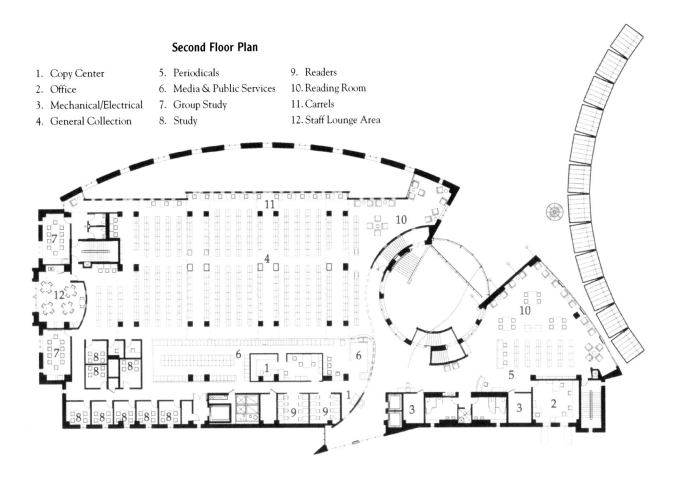

According to Jan Fox, the university's Associate Vice President for Information Technology, the library provides an environment where "students, faculty, staff, and the community can join with colleagues beyond the campus, developing and testing new visions of the learning community, exploring teaching, research, service, collaboration, and other areas." While the library allows those who use it to reach far beyond its walls, the architect's use of light and color make this building unlike any other on campus. While technology will surely change, those qualities will remain.

Curvilinear forms mark circulation systems.

the academic librarian

The John Deaver Drinko Library at Marshall University was designed to make a statement. The planning document for the building, prepared by the library planning consultant, David Kaser, in cooperation with the library staff and university administration, states that the building program:

> ...is now a welcome opportunity for Marshall University to avail itself of an occasion to construct a new building to meet its future information needs through the declining years of the codex book and into the expanding years of the electronic record....It should construct a building able from the day it opens to meet both the traditional and the advanced information needs of at least the first five years, but with the calculated and in-built capacity to modify it perhaps every five years thereafter as the scholarly migration from the printed to the electronic record gathers pace.

In other words, this library would be a showcase of new technology, while simultaneously housing the remnants of print technology. The parts of the building designed to hold books would be easily convertible to electronics.

The building was also designed to make a corporate statement about Marshall University, whose Web site proclaims that the university's vision "is the commitment that Marshall is to be '*one of the most technologically sophisticated universities of its size and type in the nation.*' The library/information center project is the core of that effort." Of the five objectives listed for the building, not one includes providing space for print materials. The description of the university as "the interactive university for Southern West Virginia" clearly bespeaks both a regional pride and a determination, through the new library building, to put Marshall and Huntington, West Virginia, on the map as centers of innovative technology, learning, and library architecture.

Large windows designate offices, administrative areas, and reading rooms.

The east façade, with the entry portico.

The all-night café is seen left of the entrance. The 24-hour reading room is to the right.

It is not surprising, therefore, that the library stands out among campus buildings for its innovation. The building is confined to a rather narrow space on campus and reflects in some of its materials, particularly its use of stone and red brick on those elevations most visible from the street, the character of the older campus buildings. But its monumental main entrance, visible only from the campus side of the building and dramatically lit at night, presents to the visitor a strikingly modern departure on this otherwise architecturally-modest campus. A measure of the perceived significance of the project to the state is the fact that the funds to complete it were provided through federal legislation sponsored by West Virginia's senior senator.

The inspiration for the concept of the building came from Marshall's former president, who was convinced of the necessity for completely integrating research, scholarship, and information, with electronics as the primary or even the exclusive means of storage and distribution. His vision included the "One Room School" concept in which course content is provided via interactive distance learning to and from other higher education sites, schools, and other venues.

Opposite page:
Interior doors are closed at night to permit the Reference Reading Room to be open 24-hours.

Opposite Page:
The upper rotunda. The red form is the
lobby to the auditorium.

Obviously, given such a concept, the traditional library functions of this "library" would be seen as necessary, but temporary. Indeed, part of the design involved the permanent allocation of one-half of the library collection to storage in the old Morrow Library across campus. The latter building houses special collections and government documents. The administration's original intention was to maintain the stored parts of the general collection as closed stacks, with daily retrieval of items requested. But faculty and student pressure forced it to provide staffing by a professional librarian and a support-staff person in order to retrieve materials needed without delay. Morrow Library is presently undergoing a thorough renovation to restore it to its 1920s appearance and to provide upgraded facilities for both archives/special collections and government documents.

A view of the reference desk from the second floor.

Third Floor Plan

1. Office
2. Mechanical/Electrical
3. Storage
4. General Collection
5. Group Study
6. Study Room
7. Reading Room
8. Carrels
9. Technical Services
10. Presentation Room
11. Green Room
12. Administration

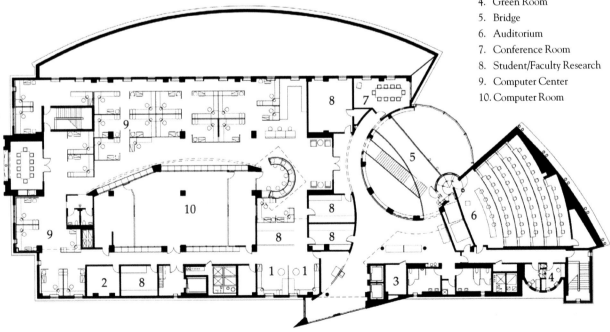

From a library perspective, the new Drinko Library is successful in a number of respects. The interactive classroom is a big success. The building is quiet, with glass and walls separating areas in order to reduce sound transmission. Light-colored walls and maple woodwork, combined with bold colors, make the building very bright. It also features an imaginative use of color. Rooms are well-designed for access to technology. The building is student-oriented. Chairs are reminiscent of a public library's. There are many pleasant reading and study nooks with nice views and comfortable chairs. There are also data-wired study rooms (for two people each; open without scheduling); team rooms with computer (for four people each; scheduled); and collaboration rooms with computer, monitor, and VCR (for ten people each; scheduled). Library office space is adequate.

The building includes three high-tech presentation rooms. Floors were built to withstand the weight of compact shelving. There is a twenty-four-hour computer and study room accessible to and from the library during regular library hours. It is open Sundays through Thursdays in the fall and spring. The room has been well-used, partly because of the closure of other facilities elsewhere on campus. There are ample public computers on floors one and three, although there is no library staff on floor three. The Current Periodicals Reading Room includes the current two years of periodicals plus microforms. Bound journals went to the stacks.

Fourth Floor Plan

1. Office
2. Hardware
3. Mechanical/Electrical
4. Green Room
5. Bridge
6. Auditorium
7. Conference Room
8. Student/Faculty Research
9. Computer Center
10. Computer Room

The Special Collections Reading Room looks out through an original door from a classroom building formerly on the site.

Opposite Page:
As one enters the campus, Marshall's "Old Main" is revealed by the curved facade.

One enters the Drinko Library through a grand atrium, flanked by a coffee shop on one side and a twenty-four-hour study/computer lab on the other. Library services are on the first two floors, with an electronic training room and consultation rooms on the first floor, and media services on the second. The third floor is divided between instructional technology and library services, while the fourth is devoted entirely to instructional technology, including an auditorium, design and test facility, computer machine room, and offices, plus faculty and student research rooms.

The Office of Information Technology, housed on the third and fourth floors, comprises three departments: Computing Services (the central computing facility for the university), Telecommunications (the central telecommunications facility for the university), and the Center for Instructional Technology. The last is the office that aims at bringing information technology to the service of the university's educational mission, supporting a variety of faculty instructional initiatives through consultation, training, and technical support.

Given the proximity of Information Technology and the Library, the vision of the former president, and the administrative organization of both IT and Libraries under a chief information officer, one would expect an integration of the staffs and flexibility in the building design, as specified by the original library building consultant. According to the university's chief information officer, who oversees these operations, integration is happening gradually over a period of years, beginning with the development of merged management teams.

In all, the Drinko Library is an impressive, user-friendly facility that achieves its purpose of making a powerful statement. Whether it truly represents the library of the future or only an attempt to promote a merger of fundamentally different types of services is yet to be seen.

Circulation desk in atrium with security gate at entrance.